Dawn: A Charleston Legend

Other works by Dawn Langley Simmons or Gordon Langley Hall:

Saraband for a Saint
The Gypsy Condesa
Me Papoose Sitter
Mrs. Weller Went to the Moon
Margaret Rutherford — A Blithe Spirit
Princess Margaret
The Enchanted Bungalow: My Grandmother, Nelly Hall Ticehurst
Golden Boats from Burma: Ann Hasseltine Judson
The Two Lives of Baby Doe: Baby Doe Tabor
Mr. Jefferson's Ladies
Dear Vagabonds: Roy and Brownie Adams, Explorers
William, Father of the Netherlands
Jacqueline Kennedy (written with Ann Pinchot)
Lady Bird and Her Daughters
All for Love
Peter Jumping Horse
Peter Jumping Horse at the Rodeo
The Great White Owl of Sissinghurst
She Crab Soup

DAWN

A Charleston Legend

Dawn Langley Simmons

WYRICK & COMPANY

For
John-Paul
who deserved better
and for
Kathleen Catalano, D.O.
whose healing hands
saved my life in 1994

Published by Wyrick & Company
1-A Pinckney Street
Charleston, S.C. 29401

Designed by Sally Heineman
Manufactured in the United States of America.

Library of Congress Cataloging-in-Publication Data

Simmons, Dawn Langley.
    Dawn, a Charleston legend / by Dawn Langley Simmons.
        p.   cm.
    Includes bibliographical references and index.
    ISBN 0-941711-16-1 : $19.95
    1. Simmons, Dawn Langley—Biography. 2. Authors,
American—20th century—Biography. 3. Transsexuals—South
Carolina—Charleston—Biography. 4. Interracial marriage—
South Carolina—Charleston.
    5. Charleston (S.C.)—Biography. I. Title.
    813' .54—dc20
    [B]
                                                              94-42517
                                                                  CIP

Contents

Foreword

In many ways, Dawn Simmons has taught me what it is to be human.

Nearly 20 years ago, Dawn came to my office in response to an ad for a writer. She was striking looking, rather slight and carried two large shopping bags filled with books, articles and magazines.

She began to tell me of her biographies on Princess Margaret and Jackie Kennedy, her adoption by Dame Margaret Rutherford, her friendship with Carson McCullers and a myriad of other luminaries. I listened to her carefully and looked at this woman who seemed so down on her luck. It was hard to believe that her life ever included the likes of First Ladies and Princesses.

She reached into the shopping bags and began to pull out books by someone named Gordon Langley Hall. There were also articles which had his name printed as author, but his name had been crossed out and replaced by Dawn Simmons' name handwritten above it. This made no sense to me—a plagiarist would have invested in whiteout.

Who sat before me? I looked into her eyes and knew that somehow everything she had told me was the truth and somewhere there was an incredible story to be told.

It begins in Heathfield England. The 15 year old daughter of an aristocrat is secretly giving birth to a child conceived at the hands of Vita Sackville-West's mechanic. The child's great aunt is dressed in black praying that this child of sin die. The young mother is clutching her baby doll as she reels in the pain of childbirth. The child is born with a deformity. Its genitals are neither decidedly male or female. In such cases according to English law the child is raised as a male. Gordon Langley Hall begins his life.

Gordon was raised by his grandmother, whose husband's death had reduced her from wealth to subsistence only six years before. She went from being in society to writing the society column in the local paper. She realized that Gordon's "terrible secret" would keep him from the joys of marriage and family, so she raised him to be a writer so that he could at least learn of life through the experiences of others.

His first poem was published when he was only four years old. By age nine he had a regular column in the *Sussex Express*. He wrote about what he knew—Vita Sackville-West, Virginia Woolf, the gypsies that camped at his grandmother's bungalow, and hundreds of human interest stories. When he was eleven he was assigned to cover Mae West's visit to Sussex. The paper sent down a professional photographer to assist its star reporter. The photographer looked all over for Gordon Hall and then realized to his surprise that Gordon was the little boy sitting on Mae West's lap on the stage conducting an interview. Gordon continued to write about his favorite subjects, unusual women.

His grandmother died when Gordon was 14. He lived on his own in small rooms, in peoples houses, in the village, doing odd jobs and writing. It was very difficult to hide his "terrible secret" amongst these strangers, so he left England for Canada where he taught Ojibway Indians on a remote reservation. He wrote his first book, *Me Papoose Sitter*, about his experiences and came to New York City to sell it. It was published and was a mild success.

One of the people who read it was Dame Margaret Rutherford, who contacted Gordon about possible movie rights. They struck up a friendship that was so deep that Dame Margaret adopted Gordon. His career flourished. He wrote for *The Boston Globe, The Herald Tribune,* and *The Winnepeg Free Press.* He covered the Royal Family for *Look Magazine* and wrote biographies and books for young adults. He moved in with an elderly cousin, the painter, Isabel Whitney and together they moved within the literary and film circles in New York City. At one reception

Gordon met Carson McCullers, who sensed something different about Gordon and said "You're really a little girl, aren't you?" At the time, he didn't know what she meant.

In 1962, Isabel died and Gordon inherited the town house, paintings, antiques, jewels and money worth 3 million dollars. He moved to Charleston, South Carolina where this "eligible bachelor" was quickly accepted into society. He restored a mansion and quietly pursued his writing. In 1967, he had started a biography of Lady Bird Johnson which required interviews at the White House.

During this period, Gordon became ill. X-rays at the hospital revealed that internally he was a woman. He went to the newly opened Gender Identity Clinic at Johns Hopkins University to begin a two year process of hormones, psychiatric counseling, and other preparations for the corrective change to a woman. The staff at the Clinic told this self-made man that to succeed as a woman he must be submissive, get a husband, give up the career and settle down to serve and be supportive to a man.

Gordon's own perceptions of women were contradictory. On one hand, he had learned of women's innermost romantic yearnings from the gothic novels he read. In these, women who were different suffered horribly and all women always suffered for love. On the other hand, the most important women in his life—Virginia Woolf, Vita Sackville-West, Isabel Whitney, and others—challenged society's boundaries for women.

As part of the Johns Hopkins program, Gordon began to dress in the gender he would become. In Charleston, Gordon was appearing as Dawn. But the Johnson book was being written as Gordon. The secret service couldn't put their finger on what was different about this guy.

The operation was complete in 1969. During the transition time a young black sculptor began a friendship with Dawn. It seemed like love at first sight for Dawn who had never experienced love. Dawn taught John Paul about art and ideas, antiques and life in society. John Paul taught Dawn about affection, spontaneity, adventure and uninhibited perception. Dawn saw John Paul as an equal and encouraged his creativity. John Paul saw Dawn as a woman with charm and grace and an uncanny humor. They were married in the first registered interracial marriage in South Carolina. The society people who had welcomed Gordon into their circle were stunned and some swore revenge.

They had to be married in Dawn's sitting room because the church had been threatened with a bomb. The insurance on the house was canceled, shots were fired into the house from the street, their dogs were poisoned and they were arrested for just walking down the street together. The pressure on them was enormous, but they both felt that they needed to stay and stand up for their love.

Dawn began to travel in order to write to support them. When she would return she would find that priceless antiques had been sold to the townspeople for a bottle of whiskey. The pressure on John Paul had caused a change in him. At first Dawn thought it was the alcohol, but later she realized it was schizophrenia. As John Paul was beginning to show signs of madness, Dawn began to show signs of pregnancy.

John Paul was hardly ever around, and Dawn's wealth was largely in the house which was sold at auction for debts. She sold a story and put a down payment on a house in a black section of town. She barely had enough to eat. She and her daughter Natasha moved into a shell of a house with 17 broken windows. Every day, John Paul's nieces would come and harass her saying "they gonna take that baby from you cause you is crazy." They thought if they threatened her child she would find some money to pay them off. Dawn was not crazy, but her emotional resources were being drained. After the murder of her last remaining dog and an attempted murder of Natasha, Dawn found refuge with Charleston's beloved Nanny, Grandmama Bernell. Dawn began to recover, but then she was told about a contract on her life.

Three years after becoming a woman, she fled Charleston with Natasha and $400 to her name. She settled in Catskill, New York and put $200 down on a deteriorating mansion. Her writing career was reduced to writing for *The National Enquirer*. She spent seven years in hunger, isolation and poverty, but never thought of herself as poor. She would collect broken objects and flowers and decorate her room with character and style. She devoted her life to Natasha and to giving her everything that money couldn't buy. She knew that she had to create a beautiful life for them.

It was about that time that my meeting with Dawn occurred and I decided to do a documentary on her life. This turned into a 7 year odyssey and a transformational experience for both of us. She regained her sense of self worth and took on writing projects which resulted in books being published. Her relationship with John Paul was changing, too. As he slid deeper into madness, she could balance her compassion for his situation with her need to protect the resurrection of her life. Natasha was her pride and joy. The nourishment of Dawn's love and teaching had overcome the sacrifices this young girl had had to make.

As I witnessed the lives in this family, I began to understand the bonds of love and something deeper that allowed the beauty in all of them to flourish—whether it was in a welfare hotel or a meadow by the river. Gordon had suffered from the isolation of being different and Dawn would not let the world repeat that on her family. Throughout the cruelest twists of fate, Dawn would always say, "That's alright dearie, it will all come out right in the end." This book is a testament to that and an insight into what it is to be human.

Dena Crane

Acknowledgements

I would like to thank Dr. Robert L. Byrd, Director of Special Collections and Curator of Manuscripts of the William Perkins Library at Duke University, for so many courtesies in supplying information from my papers there; J. John French, editor and publisher of *The Chronicle* in Charleston, whose work with me on my series *All Passion Spent; Or Is It?* sparked this book; my sister, Fay Doreen Larkin, and my school friend, Pamela Pike Standhaft Jackson, for sharing their childhood memories; my Aunty Babs (Mrs. Ernest Burgess); my daughter, Natasha Manigault Simmons; my cousins, Patricia Ivings, Nigel David Burgess, Monica Ticehurst Eaglesham, Midge Ticehurst Chisolm and Pamela Snell Lester; Nina Ticehurst Stanton; Georgia Robertson; David Shields; Marion Foster; Estella Ergle; Beryl J. Allen; Clifford R. Woolridge; Linda Ferraro; Doris Farrant Winckler; actor Robert Morley; Margaret Rummel for information on Edith Bolling Wilson; Dena Crane; Vicky Pont; Gerty Lysaght-Dunstall; my godmother, Dorrie Humphreys; Stephanie Pakosepski; Sue Bellinger; Rosabelle Waite; Florence Haskell; the Reverend Thomas Savins and his wife Margaret; Paul Bergtold; Kent Brown, a former *Post-Courier* librarian; Tina Santiago, of the Hudson Area Library, Hudson, New York; Joe Mahoney, crime editor of the *Times Union*, Albany, N.Y.; Vickie Makings, a librarian at *The Denver Post*; and my friends Jean Sherk and Janet Davis for helping to type and assemble the manuscript, together with Murray Barnes who encouraged me with his kindly counsel.

Dawn Langley Simmons,
Hudson, New York

Dawn: A Charleston Legend

Prologue

My good friend, novelist Rita Mae Brown, so aptly said, "If you take a man to Charleston and in three days he does not propose, throw him into the crape myrtle."

Sometimes I think that Charlestonians themselves are just as impulsive. In my case, John-Paul climbed up the drainpipe to the piazza of my home on Society Street, clambered through my bedroom window and awoke me from a deep sleep shouting, "Get the license. We are being married tomorrow." As Mr. James, the butler who ran the household (including me), saw fit to pronounce, "That Big Shot is something else. That's my day for polishing your door knocker."

As nobody dared go against Mr. James, who was well aware that he was one of the most respected butlers in the "Holy City," even "Big Shot" was obliged to wait. He would have had to anyway; the next day was President Richard Nixon's inauguration, so the Court House was closed. Next morning, I was received personally by Judge Gustave H. Pearlman, who was Jewish, with the greeting, "I have always been in the minority. Welcome to the minority."

He then proceeded towards two steel filing cabinets, one marked WHITE and the other BLACK. Then, with a rather wicked look in his eyes, he told me, "Now, I suppose I'll have to start another one for you." John-Paul was black. I was white.

The year was 1969, the Civil Rights decade. In its own way this union of the races that would so shock Charleston's society would play its part. It was the first legal mixed marriage in South Carolina.

What the people who so opposed our marrying did not consider was that, being British, I was obeying the Church of England whose rules are inviolate. One didn't live in sin. And as my adoptive mother, Dame Margaret Rutherford, said, "A man worth lying down with is worth standing up with." In a lighter tone, to *Time* magazine she quipped, "Oh, I don't mind Dawn marrying a black man, but I do wish she wasn't marrying a Baptist."

I was to marry John-Paul Simmons twice, in the two places I consider the most beautiful on earth—Charleston, South Carolina and the ancient town of Hastings, England overlooking the English Channel.

When Mother Rutherford found out that I had been forced to marry John-Paul in my drawing room because somebody had threatened to bomb the church, she was furious. She got the Archbishop of Canterbury out of bed at four in the morning, and shortly afterwards a second ceremony with organ and bells was solemnized in St. Clement's Parish Church at Hastings.

News about this second wedding appeared as a story in the Charleston newspapers. (The first wedding had merited a notice among the obituaries.) A German magazine, *Neue Revue*, paid my mother £30,000 for exclusive photographic rights. One editorial in a South Carolina newspaper spoke of my "illiterate negro husband." I smiled, for that same "illiterate negro husband" had sat next to the Archbishop of Canterbury, Primate of All England, at a wedding breakfast and prompted His Grace to fits of laughter. As with his marriage proposal, John-Paul was never one to mince matters. With a childlike simplicity he was always outspoken.

Growing Up In England

"It shall sweeten and make whole
Fevered breath and festered soul."
Rudyard Kipling

I remember Virginia Woolf arriving at Sissinghurst Castle swinging a large china basin by a knotted linen cloth. It was a pond pudding for Vita Sackville-West's lunch.

I was a child. Seeing me standing there—for she liked children—Mrs. Woolf asked me what I was going to be when I grew up. Without any hesitation I replied, "A writer."

"Oh," she said. Then with a twinkle in her eyes, she walked off in the direction of her friend Vita's sitting room in the tower.

Once described as the "longest love letter in history," the novel Orlando, which Virginia wrote, depicted Vita as the hero/heroine, showing over the centuries how the boy, Orlando, changed into a beautiful woman. Had she lived a little longer, Vita would have been intrigued to know that the child Dinky, as she called me, would become a real-life Orlando.

In 1943, when I was six, Vita and Harold Nicolson, her diplomat-writer husband, told me that a writer first has to learn how to research, which meant applying one's bottom to the seat of a chair. Vita also read my first manuscript, "My Cottage by the Sea," a poem I wrote that same year. It was later published in the *Sussex Express and County Herald*.

The centerpiece of Sissinghurst Castle was the red brick tower that glows sugar pink in the setting sun. Every morning, Vita, the most disciplined of writers, retired to her sitting room in the tower to write. Pictures of Virginia and the Bronte sisters, taken from a painting by their brother Branwell, shared pride of place in that lovely Tudor room with small treasures collected from childhood and in Persia, set out on fragments of faded red velvet. There were vases of blossoms, freshpicked from the garden which was destined to become one of England's most famous.

One might add that, in view of everything written of their relationship since their deaths, Vita and Virginia were lovers. Vita had many such relationships during her lifetime, her most publicized being with Violet Trefusis, which her son Nigel Nicolson describes in his book, *Portrait of a Marriage*, and which has since been the subject of a recent British television miniseries. Vita's open marriage to Harold Nicolson was, in spite of everything, a very happy one. Harold lived in London during the week, but returned to his wife and Sissinghurst for the weekends.

My natural parents Jack Copper and Marjorie (Margie) Hall Ticehurst came from different social worlds; but opposites have the habit of attracting one another. They could not live with or without each other. Their love-hate relationship would, in the end, destroy them both as all the strife and tension took its toll. It was a terrible love.

A star football player with more than his share of good looks, Jack was a wizard with the insides of a car. He was training at Major Demsey's garage to be a qualified mechanic. The youngest son of Isabella Brignell and John Copper, he was the darling youngest child of his mother's second marriage. Spoiled silly, he had won numerous prizes in Sunday school for his knowledge of the Bible, and by the time he was 19 years old, in 1937, had achieved the dubious distinction of getting three girls *enceinte* during the same period of time. One of them was Margie.

The Coppers had not always been poor, as my Uncle George Copper would point out with that little bit of snobbery so prevalent in the British working class. Then, as proof, he would show us the expensive tombstones in Burwash churchyard.

John Copper, Jack's stubborn father, had worked for a time in the early 1930s as a gardener at Bateman's, the home of Rudyard Kipling. Any Sussex-born knew that shallots, an onion-like bulb, by tradition were planted Good Friday, so when *The Jungle Book* author ordered him to plant them two weeks early, old John exploded. He crowned Kipling with the box of shallots. Then, vowing to get even, he marched off.

At his next job—village gravedigger—John Copper divided the dead into two bizarre categories, friends or enemies. The friends he buried on high, dry ground while he planted the others in the low-lying damp. For Kipling, he reserved the wettest grave in Burwash churchyard. As Grandmother Isabella kept telling him, "Don't count your chickens before they are hatched." She was right; when Rudyard Kipling finally expired in 1936, his body was cremated.

Margie, in her short life (she was 15 when she met Jack), had known better times. When her jolly, easy-going father broke his neck in a tragic fall from a horse one Christmas Eve, she saw Beecholme, the family estate at Old Heathfield, sold almost immediately. Even the beloved family nurse had to go. Though still a child, she retreated into her own world of fantasy, peopled by such characters as those found in the classics, *Jane Eyre* and *Wuthering Heights*. As Vita Sackville-West once told me, "Mrs. Copper has a wicked sense of humor. She can tell a story better than anyone. I wish she would take pen to paper."

Margie's younger sister, Gwendoline Martha, known in the family as Babs, and their cousin, Ronnie Ticehurst, were well aware of Margie's vivid imagination. Her tales of witches, goblins and haunted mausoleums half scared them to death.

When Margie's pregnancy by Jack Copper was discovered, it sent her family into turmoil. While those on her mother's side, with their hot Latin blood, were a little more worldly, the Ticehursts were not. Practicing Strict Ebenezer Baptists, they believed that children born out of wedlock were fruit of the devil. Her brother Edward Archibald Ticehurst, 18 at the time, kicked her in the stomach. She always believed that brutal incident had something to do with the way I looked when I was born. Shunned and bewildered, Margie shut herself in a darkened room for most of the long nine months.

When I finally arrived, at home, in my Spanish great-grandmother's curtain-hung bed with only a country midwife in attendance, my clitoris was so swollen that the startled woman did not know whether I was a boy or a girl. In those days, when in doubt, the unfortunate child was automatically registered male, often with dire results. I was named Gordon.

Years later, December 10, 1971, in the London Daily Telegraph Magazine, one of Britain's most reputable newspapers, writer Wendy Cooper explained how such unfortunate things happened. Today, most babies are born in hospitals where any uncertainty would be cleared up almost immediately.

Miss Cooper wrote of a spectrum of genetics that makes each of us, by varying degree, male or female:

> For most of us, where the computer has worked correctly, the criteria are concordant and we fall within the normal range toward one end or the other of the spectrum. After that everything is simple. The vital word "male" or "female" is duly entered on our birth certificate and upbringing, conditioning and training directed toward reinforcing our gender role—trousers and trains for boys, dresses and dolls for girls, and soon puberty to ram it home with physical changes.
>
> That is how it should be, but for others less fortunate it can be a very different story. Computer failure at some stage may doom them to life in the somber realm of intersex, where they must struggle with their different physical or mental sexuality in a world that, until recently, had no real understanding of

the condition, the causes or the consequences.

In the past, also, nature's mistakes were too often compounded and made worse by man's. It was all too easy for the baby born with an enlarged clitoris and no obvious vagina, to be wrongly assigned as a boy by some busy midwife or doctor, who might never have seen a similar case before. Such a mistake would then often only be discovered at puberty, when the "boy" began to menstruate.

Sometimes it could take even longer to find out, as for Gordon Langley Hall, the adopted son of Margaret Rutherford, forced to struggle with life as a man for nearly 30 years. Finally, in desperation, he went for investigation to the Gender Identity Clinic at John Hopkins Hospital, Baltimore. There the chromosome sex was firmly established as female, and ovaries and a concealed vagina revealed. After hormone treatment and surgery, Gordon emerged as Dawn to a new and far happier life, in which she not only married John-Paul Simmons but conceived and bore a child, and is now pregnant again.

In 1937, for three days and nights, Margie battled milk fever after my unwelcome arrival while her Aunt Elsie Ticehurst sat muttering how she was "a disgrace to virginhood," never herself having been with a man. In time Margie regained her strength to continue her relentless pursuit of Jack Copper, turning up at his football games with me in a baby carriage. In spite of threats from her rich Uncle George Ticehurst and prophesies of hell fire from Aunt Elsie, Margie was victorious. Asking nothing of God or man, she wed Jack Copper at Wadhurst

Registry office in 1939. Not one member of her family attended.

When my sister Fay was born, Jack was elated for he preferred girls to boys, a preference I soon noticed. Now a competent mechanic, he put his football days behind him. Loading Margie, their few pieces of furniture and my baby sister into an open lorry they set off to start a new life at Sevenoaks. My first memory is of Margie, my beautiful gentle mother, kissing me goodbye, then being driven out of my life by that awful man who happened to be my natural father. I was left behind to be raised by my grandmother.

My maternal grandmother, Nellie (she had changed her name from the more common Nelly), was no ordinary mortal. She had a Spanish mother who had spent the first 17 years of her life hidden in the Convent of the Decalced Carmelites in the fabled city of Seville, Andalusia, Spain, safe from the wrath of the Duke of Medinaceli, her father. Nellie was brought up with her twin sister, Claradoom, and older brothers and sisters at Hardwick House in the village of Groombridge, near Tunbridge Wells and close to Duckings, a half-timbered farmhouse in Withyham, Sussex, the Hall family home for centuries. My great-great-grandmother, Caroline Combridge Hall had upon her widowhood become one of the first women farmers in the county, bringing new methods and crops to her ancient lands. She was a strong woman. I always identified with her.

My other great-great-grandmother on my mother's side, the 42-year-old Condesa Elisabeta de Mendoza, who became Mrs. James Harris, arrived in the village in 1860 with her new husband who was young enough to be her son. Her daughter Marta (soon anglicized to Martha) caught the eye of Caroline's two sons, Alfred and Edwin Abraham. It was Alfred she chose, but Edwin she really loved.

Over the years Alfred and Martha made a fortune with their water mills in spite of being shunned by the neighbors who were prejudiced against Spaniards. They remembered the burning of Sussex protestants by Bloody Mary Tudor, then wed to the Spanish King Philip II. Unfazed, Martha declared, "If society will not come to me, I will make my own society," which she did until the happy day she gave birth to twins, then a rarity in Sussex. Society then came to her, first in the form of the Countess de la Warr, who arrived in her carriage to see Claradoom and Nellie, and the veil-like caul that covered the latter's little face. Others soon followed, for the caul signified the birth of a special child, one who might possess supernatural powers.

Widowed at 40 and with more money than she knew how to spend, Martha Hall moved to a fashionable villa named Fairview in Cade Street, Old Heathfield. There she designed special outfits for the twins that showed only their ankles, outfits the twins wore as they achieved local fame as female bicyclists. Cycling was a skill Nellie would put to good use later when she gathered news for her paper. Soon they were noticed by the handsome Ticehurst brothers, George and Archie, who determined to marry them. There was only one obstacle to the union; the brothers were not members of the established Church of England. Like their patriarch father, they were Strict Ebenezer Baptists. No member of the Hall family would desert the Church of England for a non-conformist.

In time, George and Archie were baptized at the font in All Saints Church with little Canon Pennethorne obliged to stand on a Jacobean chair to pour water on their foreheads.

George and Claradoom (Aunty Doom in the family) were married first, after which Archie drove Nellie home in his horse-drawn carriage, taking the wrong turn and ending up on lonely Brightling Down. Whether it was brute passion or Aunty Doom's bridal champagne I cannot say, but there among the ling heather Archie and Nellie conceived their only son, Edward Archibald Ticehurst.

Archie and Nellie were wed in a quiet ceremony. It was 1919. The bride wore gray, as British custom decreed that a non-virgin could not be married in white. As a concession, to cheer things up a bit, she wore her mother's bridal veil and Spanish mantilla. As she left from Fairview in her carriage for the ceremony, the rain poured down, while the bells that should have welcomed the happy bride sounded more like a muffled peal.

"A bad omen," said Ada Arnold who lived in a cottage by the lych-gate. It turned out she was right. Just a few years later, Archie fell from a horse and broke his neck leaving a penniless widow and three young children. Nellie never married again, even when Jim Payne, the rich undertaker, asked for her hand. "How could I," she said, "marry such a cold, cold man, when I have known what it is to be loved?"

Beecholme, a wedding present from her mother, was sold and Nellie moved into the newer part of Heathfield that had grown up around the railway station. With three little ones to raise and no money, paying guests seemed the respectable answer. When a boarder, little Freddy Shoobridge, smashed the Condesa's glass fire screen, that business venture ended abruptly.

It was then, in the mid 1930s, that my grandmother slipped into journalism. As she explained it, she knew "everybody who was anybody," so who better to write about them? Out came her bicycle upon which she set out to cover the news. Her working hat was a black astrakhan that had belonged to "poor Cousin Jack Ticehurst" who was lost in the Russian Revolution in 1917. I never did find out how he got there, but few people in that small Sussex village could boast a relative lost in something so terrible. The Bolsheviks had killed King George V's favorite cousin, the Czar, and the Russian Royal family.

Nellie, who had helped out in the days following my birth, loved to boast that at three days old, I was tied in a basket on the back of her bike as she carried me off to cover a story. Her best friend, Mrs. Kate Fox, grew tired of hearing of my early initiation into the Fourth Estate. "Nell," she quietly corrected her, "you never owned a basket in your life. That baby rode in a cardboard shoe box!"

It was Uncle George Ticehurst who built Nellie's bungalow called Havana, "with plenty of window sills for my flowers." I moved there with her in 1940, when I was three. The flowers were a great source of happiness for both of us. "I married the wrong sister," George often told Nellie. Aunty Doom was an introvert with no interest in a social life or clothes. Her greatest loves were historic houses and antiques. Her twin sister Nellie was life and laughter, an extrovert just like George.

Aunty Doom wore mousy brown and a string of big amber beads. Nellie liked color and was always clothes conscious. Even in mourning, her black and white outfits were stunning, and she could trim a hat like a professional milliner.

Poor Aunty Doom, Nellie's identical twin, never looked happy. She lived in a mansion filled with priceless antiques, but empty of love. With her dowry as seed money, Uncle George purchased one stately home at a time, restored it, then resold it at a profit. Aunty lived for her furniture, concocting a polish of beeswax and lavender that I still use today. It was she who early gave me my love for antiques and fine works of art.

Her drawing room was ethereal with a snow white carpet, and real white roses framed the French windows leading into the manicured garden. A white ribbon was hung in front of the door so that none might enter that shrine. Only once do I remember the room being used, when the Bishop of Chichester dropped by for tea, Uncle having presented him with an Old Master oil painting for his private chapel.

Aunty Doom drank coffee while others drank tea, a habit formed with her Spanish mother. Her home, Eldon House, always had that lovely aroma of coffee beans.

As for Uncle George, tall, military-like and an officer in World War I, he kept a young girlfriend named Maisie. When he died suddenly, Aunty made me search among the wreaths laid out in neat rows on the lawn to see if "that Maisie" had sent one. Maisie had not, so I did not have to throw it in the dustbin as Aunty Doom had instructed me. Aunty, now the richest of widows, refused to follow the coffin to Heathfield Church.

"I am not a hypocrite," she told her twin sister. "You must go for me. The vicar will never know the difference."

"Jolly good show," said my grandmother. "I have always wanted to be chief mourner at a military funeral." And so she was, right down to her crepe mourning veil.

It was a bit confusing for the other children who thought that I had three mothers—my grandmother and Aunty Doom who were look-alikes and the beauteous young woman who arrived once a year from Sevenoaks for a few days holiday. I called grandmother Nellie, "Mummy," and my real mother, "Margie." She was a great beauty, sweet and gentle and kind. Her visits were fleeting. After she was gone I printed by hand all the wonderful stories she told me. As a child I could not comprehend her loneliness, living as she did among the thick chestnut woods of Bailey's Hill, Sevenoaks, where Jack was chauffeur to old Mr. Wilkinson. She would go away and leave me again. She was always leaving me. As sweet revenge I decided never to kiss her goodbye. I was grown and living in America before I could bring myself to kiss her on the lips. How she must have suffered in silence.

Hanging over all my childhood like a dark pall was my physical condition. As the village stationers, Ivy and Elsie Nias, said often of the small child with the mass of golden curls, "Dinky looks just like a pretty little girl!" But then Dinky was a little girl, although my grandmother and Margie guarded the awful family secret as though it were some holy grail. School was a catastrophe, for the deformity was so noticeable where it mattered that I could not even use the public washroom facilities like the other boys at the local Church of England school. Luckily, I lived close by.

In time my voice refused to break as the other choir boys' did. I still sing soprano to this day. Then when I was between 12 and 14 there were irregular bleedings that were, as Aunt Gertrude Hall the Terrible ordered me, "to be bravely borne in secret like having an insane relative that you never talk about." (Shades of her unfortunate brother-in-law, Uncle Alfred, languishing in Hellingly Asylum where she had hidden him.) "Think of the disgrace you would be to all of us if anyone found out," she roared, her voice like the church organ. "Particularly me, as head of the Mothers Union."

There was one in the family who truly loved me, having lost both her baby boys at birth. She was my cousin Rosy, "a rough diamond," as Margie so often said, "but a diamond nevertheless." Unsinkable, she rode her own motorbike, married a man who collected steamrollers and, according to her Aunt Elsie Ticehurst, did a most unladylike thing when she joined the local fire brigade. There on the front of the big red fire truck, perched proudly beside her, I was the envy of the other children, as with bells a-ringing we sped through Heathfield High Street en route to her farm at Cade Street.

"When I grow up, you are going to be my bridesmaid," I told Cousin Rosy, and although I knew she didn't believe me, I meant it.

Little wonder that I lived in the pages I wrote. As a teenager, I worked on a novel and several short stories, including one called "Love Affair" about a vicar's seductive wife named Cora, who ran off with an insurance man. (For some unknown reason I was very hard on the clergy, who in my little stories usually had unfaithful wives. In my stories, I could always be the "heroine," fearing nobody, perpetually looking for my fairy prince.) I looked forward to holidays at Sissinghurst in spite of Jack Copper who made no bones about not liking me. There at the Tudor Castle where eccentricities and strange unnatural loves seemed perfectly normal, I did not feel so out of place. Even as children, Fay and I were aware of the gossip about how "that terrible Mrs. Woolf" had had a lesbian affair with Vita, out of which Virginia's novel, *Orlando*, had evolved with photographs of her lover as illustrations.

Orlando, when I read it (for the local library allowed me to take out grownup books) gave me a strange, new courage. Didn't my grandmother always dismiss any major problem with the sage-like words, "But it will all come right in the end." Besides, the Hall family motto was "Nothing is impossible with the Lord."

Jack first met Vita Sackville-West during his Sevenoaks years when she had a home called Long Barn at the Weald. He was soon taking care of her car in the evenings. All his life he smelled like an advertisement for carbolic soap, which must have pleased Vita who had once complained, "My God how workmen smell. The whole house stinks of them."

As their working relationship flourished, she told him that she had bought a ruined castle at Sissinghurst and would be needing a full-time chauffeur. Would he like the job, she asked, adding that it was "until the Income Tax goes up." Three decades later, "my wicked old Copper" as she called him, was still in Vita's service, pushing her around Sissinghurst in her final illness, as she rode, "like Queen Victoria."

Jane Brown tells us in her admirable *Vita's Other World*, which chronicled the making of Vita's famous garden at Sissinghurst Castle, that when Harold Nicolson and Vita moved to Sissinghurst, "Harold, having given up journalism and Mosley's politics, had no job nor expectation of any and found it frustrating trying to convince Vita that they were poor."

It was rather ironic then that their new chauffeur's wife's closest uncle and aunt were rich enough to purchase Heronden Hall in nearby Tenterden together with another large estate, Hadlow Grange, in Sussex.

As for the tower clock, Jane Brown says that it, "like so much of Sissinghurst's routine, was cared for by the faithful Copper."

My natural father had learned early in his relationship with Vita Sackville-West the fine art of being indispensable. He refused her nothing, even when she sent him down to Romney Marsh to examine some gates on a pouring wet day, nearly giving him pneumonia. In addition to his chauffeur duties, he soon became a sort of general factotum. He cared for her flock of Jacob's Sheep, buried her beloved dogs, making their tombstones, and managed to have his finger in every castle pie.

Margie's passion for her husband cooled noticeably when he brought her to Sissinghurst. "My prison," she called it. At 22, she had undergone a hysterectomy. She would always look waiflike and pathetically young. She made no bones about it, she was desperately lonely in her cottage at the castle as the dozens of letters she wrote to me reveal.

The marriage that had begun with so much passion turned into a hell on earth for both of them, with my unfortunate sister the buffer between them, for I visited Sissinghurst infrequently. Once, meeting me on the grounds, Vita remarked, "I don't think they quarrel so much. Do you think that Mrs. Copper married beneath her?" Several wealthy members of her family thought she did. When Cousin Marcus Butler had business withCaptain Oswald Beale at Castle Farm within shouting distance of the Copper home, he did not trouble to visit her. "I thought it kinder to remember Marjorie as she was," he told his mother, my great-aunt Alice Hall Butler.

Better known in the family as Aunty Dutch, Alice Hall Butler always was the grand lady. She wore a tiara to the opera and the first high-heeled shoes I had ever seen. The latter caused her to bog down in the muddy garden at Havana. My grandmother hollered, "Jump for your life." She did, landing on the tiled porch in her silk stockinged feet, leaving her shoes behind her.

For years, Aunty Dutch tried to marry off her large mannish daughter Cicely Madge to every eligible curate, doctor or lawyer in Sussex. She finally had to admit that the poor girl was a lesbian. Aunty Dutch then had the audacity to blame Virginia Woolf and the Tunbridge Wells Public Library for the copy of *Orlando* that found its way into Cicely's hands.

The classics which she had read over and over were still Margie's closest friends. At times she even saw Heathcliff in her Jack. One day Winnie Macmillan, Vita's secretary and erstwhile lover, saw fit to tell Margie that in her employer's new novel, *The Devil at West Ease*, published only in America, that she, "Mac," was the Devil, "And you are Mrs. Gartacre," she confided to a very sensitive Margie, "the neurotic wife of the vicar who spends most of her days upstairs."

Margie blossomed when I arrived to stay with them, although Jack completely ignored me. Fay and I had an exceptional relationship, exchanging a four-page magazine written with our favorite red ink, during the long weeks we were apart. There were illustrations, too. We liked to draw our romantic Aunty Babs' frilly drawers.

All through my childhood when calamity struck in the family, the cry went out, "Send for Nell." It was with some misgivings then that we set off for Birdsgrove, the villa where Aunty Doom always said the birds were too frightened to sing.

We all feared red-haired Aunt Gertrude, the childless wife of jolly Uncle Jimbo Hall. Years before, the then-17-year-old twins were to have been bridesmaids at Gertrude and Jimbo's wedding in Bexhill Parish Church. No other family members could go, for at home the twins' younger brother, Edwin, lay dying from heart disease.

The bride-to-be, a well known milliner, so intimidated Nellie and Doom, they were about to catch the next train home. However, Gertrude Geary was their match. She locked them in their bedroom.

Knotting bedsheets together, they made their escape from a window, their bridesmaids' gowns left on the bed. The twins always maintained that brother Jimbo would have joined them if he hadn't been locked up with his best man, the brother of the bride. So Aunt Gertrude and Uncle Jimbo were married, but she never really forgave the twins.

So when the messenger arrived with the news that Aunt Gertrude was dying, my grandmother said, "Blood is thicker than water. Jimbo needs me. I have to go."

We arrived to a great commotion. Aunt Gertrude's heart attack had been so bad that X-rays had to be taken in her own bedroom, then developed in the neighboring bathroom. Uncle Jimbo was told to prepare for the worst. Aunt Gertrude had slipped into a coma.

"Well," said my grandmother to Jimbo, "is there anything you fancy for supper?" for the Halls loved their food and never let a crisis affect their stomachs.

"Cheese, Nell, cheese. Toasted cheese. She hasn't given me that since the day we were married."

We were soon seated around Aunt Gertrude's polished dining table that had once been the Condesa's, each with a plate of cheese on toast. Uncle Jimbo was like an excited child. He was ecstatic.

"She'll never find out, will she?" Even then he wasn't sure liberation was nigh.

"Don't worry, she's dying."

Hardly had my grandmother spoken when an ominous voice came down from above. "Cheese, I smell cheese."

Well, to make a long story short, Aunt Gertrude recovered, outliving the rest of her generation "Nobody dies unless he or she wants to," she announced, then had her bed moved down into the drawing room where, dressed all in purple right down to the last hair ribbon, she reigned like a queen.

She ran the parish from her bed and the vicar as well. She is on record as arranging the first cremation in the village. She had the ashes of the deceased, a well-known lemonade manufacturer, brought back to her bed in a polished oak casket. Fascinated, I watched as she taped purple pansies on top. Then off to St. Richard's Church the undertaker carried it. An hour later he was back to say he had a church full of people, the organ going full blast and no vicar to officiate.

Aunt Gertrude sent for the police with instructions that the aged vicar had to be taken, by force if necessary, to the delayed funeral service. They found the Reverend Grahame Clark in a tree picking apples behind the Old Heathfield vicarage. He had completely forgotten.

It takes somebody who is disabled to recognize another, so my bond with great-uncle George Ditch was a close one. Uncle Ditcher, as we called him, was the beloved husband of great-aunt Elizabeth Hall Ditch. He made me feel special. When I was between the ages of nine and twelve years old, he planned a fresh project every Saturday for me to carry out. It might be to sketch an old Roman fort, or an expedition to explore lonely Bodiam Castle; off I was sent on my bicycle. Back at Spicers for tea, I recounted my adventures while he listened from his big oak arm chair drawn up close to the table.

Spicers, the Ditch home on Cade Street in Old Heathfield, was a magical house dating from Tudor times with its own secret passage that led to a small hidden room. There Catholic priests had been hidden from the wrath of Elizabeth Tudor. I had explored that old house many times without discovering its secret. How grownup I felt when on my eleventh birthday Great Aunty Liz showed me the panel with its winding staircase behind. "It is my present," she said, "our secret."

Aunty Liz would never get married, the Hall family thought, but she had other ideas. She first met Ditcher in a library at Hailsham. They courted in secret, then wed in Old Heathfield Church after which he made her Mine Hostess at Chiddingly's Eight Bells Inn. Later moving to the Dicker, a neighboring village, Uncle invented a fizzy drink called "Monsters," and predicted a fortune from its sale. The promising venture ended abruptly when Uncle, out rabbit shooting, tripped over his gun. The gun went off, shooting him in the hand and spine. He became paralyzed from the waist down. The couple retired to Spicers to continue their now curtailed lives, but how they lived!

Theirs was the open door through which one never knew who would pass—politicians and gypsies, relatives and clergy. To a youngster growing up the conversation was an education in itself. "Let the child speak," Uncle would bellow while I tangled with the Bishop of Lewes as to whether King Canute's daughter was really in that stone coffin they had discovered in Bosham. "Remember we have to pass on the torch to the next generation."

Aunty Liz wore the shortest of dresses, her black-ribbed stockings rolled down to the knee. A wisp of fine lace was glimpsed at her breast, and at a time when women of her age didn't smoke, she used a long amber cigarette holder. With her gray hair in a bun, Aunty Liz, helped by their bald-headed maid, Kitty Scott, who wore a small knitted cap, made Cuckoo Fair Day the best day of the year.

Cuckoo Fair had been held at Heathfield, formerly Heffle, since medieval times. Legend said that the cuckoo was first heard on the first of April when the bird escaped from a woman's basket. By my time, the fair had become a horse and cattle show held in a field opposite Spicers behind the Half Moon Inn. In the long lane gypsy youths from all over England proudly raced their ponies while we cheered them on, led by Uncle Ditcher who was carried outside for the fun.

All day long Kitty served refreshments—chicken, baked ham, meat pies, cheese pies, apple tarts—all to be washed down with gallons of cold cider and hot tea. Kitty was a character in her own right, just as outspoken as her employers. When some wandering gypsy told Uncle that rubbing the scalp with a raw onion induced hair to grow, there was no peace until he tried the remedy on Kitty. My grandmother said he should have left well enough alone for when the hair grew just as the gypsy had predicted, it was a flaming shade of red just like Aunt Gertrude's.

General elections were also exciting as Uncle backed the Labor party and Aunty the Conservative party. Both fought over Kitty's vote. Everybody laughed when husband and wife each engaged a taxi to take Kitty to the polls and both taxis arrived at the same time. It was Kitty herself who solved the problem, announcing she would go to vote in one, then return to Spicers in the other. Although Uncle and Aunty and Kitty Scott were all long gone when I married, Kitty's cousin, Elsie Carter, attended my second wedding ceremony at Hastings. Mrs.

Carter remembered that red hair well.

Our life at Havana, the bungalow my grandmother had named for a Cuban cigar, went quietly on as I learned how to live with my physical condition. I spent ages 3-12 there. Proficient in botany, my grandmother introduced me early to the naming of wildflowers. The local horticultural society show had special children's classes. For my knowledge of wildflowers and grasses I won prizes and pocket money for the year. Bird watching, local history and writing completed my world.

We had a cat, named Charmaine, given us by cousin John Holland, who would live to be 20, and a chinchilla rabbit named Molly who was also a prizewinner. A pet chicken called Moonyeen sat in a wicker chair on the porch. Moonyeen was no ordinary bird. She was rescued, saved featherless from Charles, Aunty Babs' amorous rooster, and carried home to Havana in a Christmas cake box. Everybody laughed when my grandmother bought six eggs from Mr. Bannister the grocer for Moonyeen to hatch in her chair on the porch. But in due time, two baby chicks were hatched from the six eggs, a Rhode Island Red and a White Leghorn. My grandmother's comment was: "You see, even a store hen can make a mistake."

Into our quiet lives, at about this time, came Pamela Pike, a native of Eastbourne, a town on the Sussex coast. I travelled there daily to attend school, where Pamela and I met in history class. Pamela was hooked on archaeology. Her wonderful father took us for digs on the South Downs. Pamela's great love was, and still is, ancient Egypt which was all my grandmother needed to hear. Pamela must give a talk at Heathfield's Agricultural Hall.

Pamela duly arrived looking very grownup, wearing a large floppy hat. I was more nervous than she. How those church ladies loved her. You could have heard a pin drop, so quiet were they. "Better than a church sermon," Elsie Carter said, after listening to Pamela's recipe for embalming a mummy.

My close friendship with Pamela, now Mrs. Dennis Jackson, of Romsey, Hampshire, in England, has endured to this day.

Pamela belonged to the happier days of childhood. I liked being part of the Pikes, whom I considered "a normal family." However, even the time I spent with her family could not dispel the disgrace of illegitimacy, of which pious church-going old women and the Ticehurst Strict Ebenezer Baptist great-aunts constantly reminded me. It didn't make any difference to them that my parents had long since married and I had my father's name on my amended birth certificate.

Only once do I recall my grandmother weeping and that was when the new curate called all in a dither. I was to be confirmed, yet he could find no record of my baptism. I had been baptized at St. Bartholomew's Cross-in-Hand Church with Margie's best friend, Dorrie Humphrey, as godmother, and it should have been recorded in the church register there. To this strange young man my grandmother had to unfold the sad tale of my birth. Although my parents had married, making me legitimate, nobody had thought to change the baptismal entry. I was still listed as Ticehurst.

My grandmother always had enjoyed such good health that when at 60 she began to fail it seemed all so unreal. She was suffering from terminal breast cancer. In 1949, Margie came home and together we nursed her. It was a horrible time. The memory of blood stained sheets in the bathtub will always be with me.

The night that Grandmother died, Margie ran from the house while I stayed in my room watching a strange blue light that encompassed the mantlepiece. Grandmother was buried on a foggy December day in the same grave as her young husband. We had sung "Fight the Good Fight," the Hall family hymn, then followed the white oak coffin surmounted by a bronze cross down to the churchyard.

Havana was sold. I was homeless. I cycled to my grandmother's grave and wept.

The contents of Havana were sold at Heathfield Market. There is nothing so sad as seeing much loved possessions lying discarded as dead soldiers after a battle. Even her precious portrait of her close friend Lord Baden Powell, the founder of the Boy Scouts, was there—it had always hung over her bed. In this case my grandmother's long battle was over; mine had begun.

At age 12, with no home and a father who didn't want me, I turned as I always have to my church where a rich old lady, Jessie Mountain, took me in. She lived alone in a red brick pre-Raphaelite house with William Morris wallpapers. I retained my independence by taking up some of my grandmother's newspaper reporting and helping a nice lawyer named Shirley S. Hodson in his office (I did the old English lettering on deeds, wills and indentures). My ambition was still to be a writer; I was working on a novel in which Margie came through thinly veiled as the beauteous mother, with me the ugly unwanted child.

Still hanging over me was that same deep, dark secret of my true identity. Always I wished it would vanish like a bad dream, but it didn't. With the exception of dear old Pamela and Tony Stapley, a local boy who shared my affinity for animals and whose mother had gone to private school with the Hall twins in Royal Tunbridge Wells, there were no other close relationships with my peers. There couldn't be. For my part I was mortally afraid of anything physical. I put all thought of sex out of my mind. Besides, those bleedings were frightening.

Uncle Ditcher was carried into Heathfield churchyard not long after my grandmother, and Aunty Liz disbanded Spicers. His death left another void in my life. Aunty Liz went to live with her son George Alfred Hall Ditch, whose nice wife Lily gave her breakfast in bed every day for the rest of her life.

Aunty Doom moved to Royal Tunbridge Wells where she lived out her life as a happy rich widow at Sandrock House, once home to her own grandmother, the Spanish Condesa. In Heathfield where I lived in an apartment called St. Anthony's, only Uncle Jimbo and Aunt Gertrude remained. I was 15 when I was summoned to Birdsgrove to help with preparations for their golden anniversary.

Aunt Gertrude, who had not officially left her bed for years (although there were those who were sure she walked through the rooms every night), decided on the great day to receive the gentlemen of the press, eager to see what the legendary Mrs. Hall looked like. They were surprised, for Aunt Gertrude, who used no cosmetics except face powder, was remarkably well preserved, her untinted hair still flaming red. She wore a French nightgown of purple crepe-de-chine with hair ribbons to match.

We perched poor fat Uncle on a slipper chair by her bed for photographs. Then suddenly, without warning, Aunt Gertrude said, "Gentlemen, I've been married 50 years and am still a virgin."

Later, after a good supper of boiled beef and carrots, Uncle Jimbo died in his sleep. The question was, who would take care of his wife? They need not have worried for she had already decided. Looking me straight in the eye, Aunt Gertrude said, "You."

"Me?" I stood like somebody just sentenced to die.

"Yes, you. I know, as you know, that you are a girl."

Aunt Gertrude thought she had won, but then went too far. "I don't like dogs. You will have Freddie (my Chihuahua) put to sleep, thus as a special privilege you may sleep in your dear Uncle's bed."

What she never understood was that I, too, had a mind of my own. I went home and wrote Aunty Alice Copper Bonkowski, Jack's sister in Detroit, asking her to sponsor me so that I could emigrate to America. Then I auctioned the contents of St. Anthony's and together with the proceeds of my grandmother's small insurance policy had just enough for the fare. One sunny morning, Freddie and I slipped quietly out of Heathfield. We sailed from Liverpool to Canada, then caught the train to Detroit.

When I reached Windsor, Ontario, to cross into the United States, I was met with bad news. Uncle Walter Bonkowski had been killed by a hit-and-run driver. My sponsor was gone, and I was stranded in Canada. After finding Freddie a good home with an elderly couple who spoiled him into a good age, I took work as a teacher on an Ojibway Indian reservation at Gull Bay on Lake Nipigon where I worked for a year. Looking back, the more worldly Ojibways thought "teacher," as they called me, very young and innocent. It was 1953, and I was only 16.

There was a wonderful old lady called Poor Old Grandmother whose ambition was to have a coming out party (she was then 82) because she had been told that Princess Margaret had had one. I also met a small boy named Charley who knew everything and a femme fatale, Angelic Majada, with the proverbial heart of gold. Before the

Indian mothers went fishing through holes in the lake ice in winter, they brought their babies to the schoolhouse for me to mind. Still in the tignokens (cradle boards) they would hang them in a row from pegs set in the wall! Out of these experiences I was able to write my humorous first book, *Me Papoose Sitter* and later two children's books, *Peter Jumping Horse* and *Peter Jumping Horse at the Rodeo*.

My Ojibway days terminated abruptly when the bush plane in which I was travelling made a crash landing in a snowbank, breaking my shoulder. After a spell in a hospital run by a jovial group of nuns who only spoke French, I was determined to legally enter the United States. While waiting for my working visa I was employed first as a general reporter, then as the obituary editor for the Winnipeg *Free Press*; the latter was no easy job with so many hard-to-spell Russian and Polish surnames in that midwestern city. As the crime reporter was then living in sin with a clergyman's daughter, I often helped him at nights when he slipped home to see her. At the Winnipeg *Free Press* I received the valuable training to always meet a deadline on time.

I left the newspaper in 1955, when my working visa was finally granted. I entered the U.S. at Noyes, Minnesota, on a Greyhound bus. Through *Editor and Publisher*, I had found a job as society editor for the Nevada *Daily Mail* in Nevada, Missouri, whose able city editor, Ken Postlethwaite, taught me a lot. My first big story to go out over the wires was an interview with President Harry Truman's maiden sister, Mary Jane, who was visiting close friends in the city. When I phoned for a story she agreed on the condition I wouldn't mention politics. I didn't. My article told of Harry and Mary Jane playing piano duets together as children. From my grandmother's stint at the *Southern Weekly News* I had learned that human interest stories were always the best.

A year later, when, regretfully, I finally moved on to New York, Ken wrote in an editorial that a reader who had lived all her life in Nevada phoned in to say that I knew things about the city that even she didn't know! I have always thought that Nevada, Missouri, was the *real* America, honest and true.

In New York City, I worked as an editor with General Features, a newspaper syndicate, then, missing the excitement of a daily newspaper, with the Port Chester *Daily Item*. During this period I wrote a modern "morality" play, *Saraband for a Saint*, being my interpretation of a medieval miracle play. It was performed in the chancel of St. Martin's Episcopal Church, in New York's predominantly black Harlem. We had a professional director, Kim Andrews. The story was about two young soldiers, one British and white, the other American and black. I had never been to the Deep South where one scene was set, so I was totally ignorant of the role it was soon to play in my personal life. The action took part in a bombed Italian church during World War II where, seeking shelter, the two men recall their lives. The theme was brotherly love. Bishop James Pike likened my writing to that of the Danish philosopher Soren Kierkegaard (1813-1855). The British soldier was filled with hate for the beautiful mother who had deserted him as a child. His black companion had, by contrast, been brought up surrounded by the love of his old grandmother who was criticized by her fellow blacks for the care she lavished on a lovely old white woman. In a flashback, the southern granny appears to say, "Everybody needs to be loved by somebody, and old Miss Abby needs me."

The two acts linking the play together were enhanced by the tenor voice belonging to Raymond Smith, a doctor with the U.S. Veteran's Administration. A man of 36, he shared his love of nature and ecology with me on Sunday afternoons, taking me for drives into the more rural parts of New Jersey. I never see a wild dogwood that I do not think of Raymond. He was a true friend, a life-long friend.

For some reason the play received much press publicity. Diverse celebrities as Joan Crawford, Helen Hayes, and boxer Sugar Ray Robinson sent their good wishes. A Broadway theater group came in, and for no recompense, wired the church for sound. And, Dr. Francis Geoffrey Fisher, Archbishop of Canterbury, invited me to Lambeth Palace to discuss the play. It was a great experience, especially when he gave me a personal tour of the palace, pointing out the portraits of his predecessors. It was history come to life. I thought how much my fellow history buff, Pamela Pike, would have loved it.

There was one funny anecdote at dinner. The dessert was a crisp caramel torte. When the Archbishop of Canterbury attacked it with his fork, it jumped right off of his plate and onto the linen table cloth. Picking it up, he looked at his wife and me. "I am going to eat this with my fingers," he said with a smile, "and I suggest that you both do the same."

The Whitney Days

"I dwell among my own people."
Inscription on crucifix,
Clovelly Parish Church,
Devonshire, England

"She is more precious than rubies."
Proverbs 3:15
(Text on Isabel Whitney's tombstone.)

S everal months later, I found myself alone in a hospital bed at St.
Luke's Hospital in New York City. I came close to despair. Just as
things seemed to go nicely, the old trouble always returned like the
plague; irregular bleedings and a terrible swelling in my belly as if I
were pregnant.

Me Papoose Sitter was under contract to T.Y. Crowell while the
Hutchinson Company was to bring out its own edition in London with
delightful cartoon illustrations by Colin Stark. I enjoyed my job as a
reporter with the Port Chester *Daily Item* where Bill Bassett, the editor,
had given me more than my share of bylines. In addition, I was also
writing feature articles for newspapers as diverse as the Boston *Globe*,
the New York *Daily Mirror* and the New York *Herald Tribune*. I had a
small apartment just off Riverside Drive where the rabbi next door was
intrigued by my knowledge of the Old Testament prophets, which I had

studied in the Church of England school.

Margie and Aunty Babs both anxiously wrote, "Come home," but would themselves have rather crossed the Atlantic in a canoe than travel by airplane. Then, too, where was home? Sissinghurst was the place for brief holidays; Jack would never have wanted me as a permanent "guest." Poor Margie, consumed by her love for him and for me, was caught between the devil and the deep blue sea. Meanwhile, between medications, I fretted by the hour. Then, one afternoon, life took on a new meaning with the arrival of the most unselfish person I have ever met, Cousin Isabel Lydia Whitney.

Looking somewhat like Queen Mary, in spite of a small lightweight crutch, hair piled high, long ruby earrings flashing, she swept into the room.

"Why didn't you tell me you were living in New York? I didn't know or I would have helped you."

I blushed. "Actually I wanted to sell my first book by myself."

"But I could have helped. I know many publishers."

"That was what I was afraid of, the illustrious name of Whitney. I would never have known if they had accepted it on its own merit."

She pondered a minute, then sat down.

"You are quite right. The name never really helped me as a painter. It was a hindrance instead of an incentive. Whenever I managed to sell a piece of my work, Mother always said that I didn't need the money. Only Dad ever said, 'Darned good.' "

Cousin Isabel left with the promise I would be hearing from her soon. After she had gone, the nurses asked if she were visiting royalty!

My family, the Halls, had retained a distant connection with Isabel's maternal family, the Hasseltines, because of what can best be described as two bizarre Victorian marriages.

Isabel's two great aunts, Sarah and Lydia Hasseltine Cummings, the latter a minor Hudson River painter, both fell in love with Hiram Coombs, an early buyer for Wannamaker's. Aunt Sarah was plain while Aunt Lydia was beautiful. When Aunt Sarah went into a then-fashionable decline and cried without stopping, Aunt Lydia announced somewhat generously, "If you want him so much, you may have him." Uncle Hiram had no say in the matter. He and Aunt Sarah were promptly wed in a Brooklyn church with Aunt Lydia serving as bridesmaid. Then they all lived together in harmony until Aunt Sarah gave birth to little Willie. This caused Aunt Lydia to pine for a child of her own, without benefit of a husband.

Then it was that Aunt Lydia travelled to London, where she contracted "a marriage of convenience" (paying a large sum for the privilege), marrying a dour looking gentleman named Edward Harris. After sitting for a wedding daguerreotype, she pensioned him off, then returned home to America, never guessing that her white satin wedding bonnet would one day form part of the costume collection in the Metropolitan Museum of Art in New York.

At Aunt Sarah's home in Brooklyn another member was added. Aunt Lydia and the absent Mr. Harris adopted her infant niece, Martha Hasseltine, from a sister who died in childbirth. Both Hiram and Sarah Marion were passive people; only once did the latter confide to her diary, "Sister dined with us last night...but then Sister always dines with us!"

To round out the story, it was Edward Harris's brother, James, who wed my flamboyant Spanish great-great-grandmother, the Condesa, when he was 19 and she 42. Again, it was a marriage of convenience. Preferring men to women, he needed an understanding wife in order to claim an inheritance, and she needed a British passport to rescue her daughter from a grim Spanish convent.

Cousin Isabel had achieved fame in her own right as America's first woman fresco painter, studying old manuscripts in the Library of Congress to learn their ancient formulae. In the 1920s, to the delight of the local tabloids, she dressed in overalls that included three-quarter length pants and climbed a skyscraper scaffold in the pursuit of her work. Ironically, a few years after the papers first carried her story, she fell off a chair on which she was standing in her own kitchen, crippling herself for life. Her fresco days over, she turned to watercolors as her favorite medium. In 1964, her work would be included in an exhibition of women artists' work from 1664-1964, held in the Newark Museum.

Her father, Joseph Botsford Whitney, had been one of the founders of the Paterson Silk Industry in New Jersey. As a cabin boy he had been on the first ship after Commodore Matthew C. Perry to enter Japan, then virtually isolated from the Western world. Then began his romance with the Far East and he returned many times in the pursuit of his calling. A brilliant Chinese robe given him by the last Empress of China would later descend to me. In turn, I gave it to the Georgia-born authoress Carson McCullers who wore it to the premiere on Broadway of Edward Albee's adaptation of her novella *The Ballad of a Sad Cafe*. Carson arrived on Mr. Albee's arm, later leaving the colorful red and blue robe to the University of Texas, Austin.

At 11 years old, Isabel was the third female ever to attend the Pratt Institute of Design in Brooklyn, a fact that earned her mother much criticism from Brooklyn society. Isabel's hair was still long, hanging down her back, when she attended life drawing classes at which both male and female nudes were used.

Both Isabel and Hasseltine, her sister, played with the future President Franklin D. Roosevelt at Hyde Park when he was a boy, complaining to their mother that Franklin was selfish as he wouldn't share his toys with them. Many years later when their parents died within a few weeks of one another, subjecting them to a doubled inheritance tax, Isabel appealed to their erstwhile playmate, now in the White House. He tried to tell her that even the President could not alter the law enacted by the New York Legislature; there was absolutely nothing he could do. Isabel was both hurt and furious. Rising to her feet in the Executive Office, she pointed her crutch at him and said, "You were always a nasty little boy and now you are a nasty old man." Isabel and Hasseltine, like their parents Joseph and Martha Hasseltine Whitney, always had a great respect for angels.

At the time of the great financial crash of 1929, Isabel's parents credited angels with saving the family fortune. Mr. Whitney dreamed that an angel ordered him to sell all the family stocks, which he did, converting them into hard cash. Two large Spanish gessoed angels on Isabel's drawing room mantlepiece commemorated the fact. Said she,

"Mother was quite embarrassed that while her friends were jumping out of windows, having lost everything, their own fortune had been miraculously saved."

The day I was discharged from the hospital, "Cleaned up for a little longer," as the doctor said, Cousin Isabel wrote me a letter on beautiful peach-colored notepaper with crinkled edges. I had given her permission to discuss my medical problems, as she already had known of the family secret concerning me.

> My dear Pet Lamb,
>
> As you are aware I live in an historic old house on West Tenth Street—alone since your cousin Hasseltine died three years ago. You do remind me so of her...the way you sit with your right hand draped over the arm of a chair, and like she, your need to be looked after and protected from a cruel world.
>
> I am getting older, although I will not tell you how old as I do not believe in a material age. My friends worry me to find an apartment but I have always lived in big houses and I'm sure that such confinement would be like a prison.
>
> I think that we need each other. I have spoken to Mr. Keeler, my attorney, and he has suggested that you live on the fourth floor of my home and be given a weekly allowance. You will be fed, clothed and have complete privacy on your floor to write. We will meet for tea every afternoon and spend Sundays and holidays together. On the advice of your physician you will terminate your position as a reporter with the Port Chester *Daily Item* and concentrate on writing books. As Father always said, "Pass on the torch!" I am glad to offer you that torch called achievement.
>
> Affectionately,
> Isabel

So with two large energetic ladies from St. Martin's Episcopal Church to direct the proceedings, I moved from West 103rd Street to the Whitney mansion at 12 West Tenth. Isabel had taken the gold family carpets out of storage, for since her accident she allowed no carpets or rugs in her suite, and had them laid on my floors. She had a wonderful storeroom filled with discarded family furnishings. A Connecticut Queen Anne table was brought up for my dining table. I was given a period Philadelphia card table to work on. I loved the acanthus carvings on the base.

My only regret was leaving the newspaper for I had been associated with newsprint all my life, starting in my grandmother's time. The managing editor of the New York *Daily Mirror* said he would gladly give me a job, but he thought I was nuts to even ask him. He wished he could just stay home and write books. So I decided to pen a book about Princess Margaret's achievements as a good will ambassadress for her sister, the Queen, and of her popular tours of Canada and the Caribbean. It was beautifully produced in an illustrated edition by the Macrae Smith Company.

The Whitney House dated from the early part of the 19th century, with a brownstone main entrance and steps together with a large crinoline window—a window seat in a bay built to accommodate enormous hoop skirts—which had been added during the Lincoln era. In that window, Emily Post, the etiquette authority, who once lived in the house, often had sat to write on good manners. The widower, President Woodrow Wilson, had once come secretly to the house to eat Thanksgiving dinner with Edith Bolling Galt, widow of Norman Galt. A new butler had substituted an ordinary china porridge bowl for the silver gravy boat and everyone was most embarrassed.

Downstairs, a Tiffany window of a berobed lady festooned with pink flowers and blue butterflies reflected the morning sunshine, while an enormous bronze of a naked man being carried off to heaven by a fierce-looking angel brandishing a sword welcomed the visitor. Isabel always hung the latchkey to her suite on one of the frightening angel's feathers.

Her own rooms were, as Alice Winchester, editor of *Antiques* mag-

azine, so aptly called, "a capsule in time with gold leaf predominating."
The 18th century French marquetry and ormolu commodes were the
legacy of her mother who had an affinity for the ill-fated Marie
Antoinette; the Belter sofas and chairs were Aunt Sarah and Aunt
Lydia's; the pair of Federal mahogany mirrors had belonged to George
Washington. They later belonged to Eli Whitney, a family member
who had invented the cotton gin, a machine for separating cotton fibers
from the seeds. We also used his monogrammed teaspoons for our
afternoon tea. Art lined the walls as in a gallery, including a Tait (Arthur
Fitzwilliam Tait, 1819-1905) and an Inness (George Inness 1825-1894),
both acquired by Isabel's father Joseph Botsford Whitney, while delicate
Satsuma porcelain picked up on his travels to Japan entirely filled one
golden gessoed china closet. A suite of furniture—sofa and chairs with
petit point embroidered backs showing "Mary and Her Little Lamb"—
is now displayed in a Victorian period room at the Brooklyn Museum.

Over the marble mantle, rescued from the old Berkeley Hotel when
it was demolished on lower Fifth Avenue, was an enormous circular
painting of Botticelli's *Angels*, which Isabel had copied while on a visit
to Germany and Russia in her youth. After World War II the original
vanished, and when Isabel's copy appeared in a magazine with the caption, "It is now believed to be in a famous American collection," she had
a good laugh. Isabel's studio was in the basement, converted from what
had been the old kitchen. There, every morning except Sunday, she
worked on her watercolors while I wrote upstairs. It was a very good
arrangement.

There were, of course, some things that took a little getting used to.
Because her father always bought 25 pairs of shoes at a time, she sent
out and did the same for me. When I bemoaned the fact that I hadn't a
good likeness of Margie, there was no peace until an artist had been
commissioned to paint her. Fortunately, it was Elena Hatfield who was
Spanish, and the resulting portrait in oils was an excellent likeness.
Isabel sent Marie Antoinette's triple diamond earrings and necklace to
be worn and, although Margie thought her bare shoulders "somewhat
indecent," the portrait was, for me at least, a great success. She looks
much taller than she really was in life due to the fact that the artist

perched her like a child on a high stool.

In spite of expensive shoes and portraits, in other ways Cousin Isabel tried, at least on the surface, to be frugal. Every night she personally darkened all the lights in the foyer and stairways to save electricity. When we went uptown for dinner or the theater, although she was dripping with jewels, we never took a taxi but always the bus. In today's crime-ridden New York with all those diamonds and rubies, we would have been shot.

Visitors to the house included: Alice Madden whose family had been connected to the founding of Woolworth's department stores; Belle Hayes, who looked like Mary Pickford and should have been an architect for she was great at building houses and creating beautiful gardens; Isabel's investment counselor William Walsh of Paine, Webber, Jackson & Curtis; and William Jenkins Foster of General Motors and his wife Marion, who had a career of her own with the Red Cross. Isabel called them "the young Fosters." She loved it when they took her out to dinner. William's mother was a Jenkins from Edisto, South Carolina. The most frequent visitor was George Keeler, her confidante and attorney who always carried a large, well-worn black briefcase. Isabel affectionately called him "my oyster."

The only time Isabel left the house overnight was for a day or two with Alice or Belle where she painted in their gardens or decorated their furniture. For a few weeks each summer she retired to the Mohonk Mountain House where she worked from nature. In 1956, I purchased Beecholme, Margie's old family home at Old Heathfield in Sussex, with the *Me Papoose Sitter* book club moneys. While Isabel was at Mohonk I visited Beecholme. This was an ideal arrangement, for as Belle Hayes said, "They are so good for each other."

The Whitney House was run by a number of old family retainers including the irrepressible Mary Janekovic, a native of Yugoslavia who, Isabel's mother decided years before, had hidden talents quite lost in her role as a maid. Her needlework was so fine that Mary was sent off to study with a well-known courtier, later becoming a dress designer. However, Mary considered it her right to serve as maid at Isabel's afternoon tea parties at which she duly appeared clad in a beige uniform and cap right out of the 1920s. There were real diamond pins pinned to her breast and the front of her cap so that one day a guest dared to ask Isabel, "Are those real diamonds Mary is wearing?" "Of course," snapped Isabel, who did not tolerate nosy people. "Mother gave them to her."

On the plump, well-fed side herself, Mary did not approve of slim ladies. She always thought they looked hungry. One tasty memory I have is of Mary pressing a rich chocolate acorn upon Marion Foster, who had what was considered a very good figure, with the words, "You are much too thin, Mrs. Foster." On Christmas Eve, Mary always arrived with the Yugoslavian cookies she had made for Miss Isabel.

Red letter days were when Pearl S. Buck, author of *The Good Earth*, came for tea and advice. She had respected Isabel's clear thinking since the days of her marriage to her publisher/mentor, Richard Walsh, after what Isabel called "a most civilized divorce" from Dr. Lossing Buck, her first husband. When she wanted an opinion from someone she could trust, she visited Cousin Isabel. Unfortunately, she didn't always let us know much in advance she was coming.

As she arrived in an enormous motor car, we were always hard pressed to find her a parking space. Once I remember how Isabel in desperation phoned the local police precinct.

"This is Miss Whitney. Pearl Buck is coming to tea and I don't know what to do with her car."

The next thing we knew a policeman turned up with a couple of signs which he placed in the street in front of our house. They read somewhat surprisingly: NO PARKING TODAY. FUNERAL.

Perhaps the most interesting visitor we had was Princess Ileana, of Romania, who later founded her own order of nuns near Pittsburgh. She was a great-granddaughter of Queen Victoria and with her husband and children had escaped from the Nazis in World War II, bringing her crown wrapped in a nightgown. This she later sold to educate her children. About the time that she visited Isabel and me, she gave a valuable religious icon to the Cathedral of St. John the Divine, New York City, in memory of her parents, King Ferdinand and Queen Marie.

During the tea, which took place in the dining room on my floor, the princess's eyes kept returning to the ruby earrings that Isabel was wearing, to say nothing of the sparkling gems worn by the maid!

When we entertained the popular novelist Frances Parkinson Keyes, our houseman, helped by two friends, carried her upstairs in her wheelchair. She was of Isabel's vintage and social background, thus tea that day sounded more like a high school reunion. When she left she invited us to visit her at her home, Beauregard House, in New Orleans. She also sent me a large autographed photograph of herself seated next to a large Scarlet O'Hara lamp. With the picture was a note from her secretary that read, "Mrs. Keyes doesn't send her photograph to just anybody."

Through Isabel's friendship with Emeline K. Paige, editor of *The Villager*, in Greenwich Village, I was to meet my childhood heroine, the movie legend, Bette Davis. Miss Davis and her fourth husband, actor Gary Merrill, were then living in Maine where Miss Paige and her lifelong friend, Janet Hutchinson, were running an inn at Camden where the film *Peyton Place* had just been made. I was invited to the premiere in Camden in 1957. Bette Davis was to be the star attraction and mistress of ceremonies.

As a child, I made scrapbooks on Bette Davis's career. Unfortunately for Miss Davis, whose eldest daughter, B.D., had attended school with Janet Hutchinson's son, Jefferson, Hollywood failed to produce the "stars" she was to introduce at the premiere, so all she had to work with was the "Donut Queen of Maine" and myself. This did not faze Miss Davis at all. "They shall have their parade," she said. She, the Donut Queen and I rode together in a limousine.

Miss Davis said she was very touched when she found out about my scrapbooks. In later years, she was morally supportive of me. I liked Gary Merrill, too, although I felt saddened when in the course of conversation Miss Davis asked, "Which were your favorites among my old movies?" Before I had time to reply he quipped, "*I don't have any old movies.*" There was a moment of hurt in his famous wife's famous eyes.

I had bought small gifts for Miss Davis's three children, B.D., Margo and Michael. She looked so pleased. "Most people forget Margo," she said, smiling. Margo, named for her mother's famous screen role in *All About Eve*, was mentally retarded.

Back at the Whitney House, I could credit Isabel with my knowledge of American history that was to result in my writing several biographies over the years that have followed.

Her interest, her firsthand experience and her ancestry were an inspiration. Isabel's forebears were part of that history, persons such as Eli Whitney. "Just look at his face," she once exclaimed. "See! He has the high Whitney forehead, all right for a man but a handicap to a woman like me." She saw me look first at Eli's portrait then at Isabel's own forehead with the row of neat little bluish-gray curls. I gasped when she removed them all with a sweep of her hand.

"Pure vanity," she said, "Pure Whitney vanity."

On her mother's side had been Ann Hasseltine, the first of Adoniram Judson's wives, who gave her young life willingly for her missionary husband's work. She was the first American woman to live in Burma—a similar situation to that of Anna with the King of Siam. Adoniram was imprisoned for several months for trying to convert the King's people to Christianity. Ann's agile mind charmed the King of Burma, even though she defied him by sending her imprisoned husband messages hidden in a teapot spout. The King enjoyed talking with Ann on a variety of subjects, especially America. Isabel's family credited her with saving Adoniram's life. Ann died April 26, 1826, of a tropical fever. She was 36.

Men in Isabel's family had fought on opposite sides in The War Between the States. "Brother against brother," Isabel told me. In her own time, her cousin Gertrude Vanderbilt Whitney, a talented sculptress, had founded the Whitney Museum. Isabel's most famous living cousin was John Hay Whitney, American ambassador to Great Britain in 1962.

Martha Hasseltine Whitney, flanked by her daughters, Isabel and Hasseltine, marched down Fifth Avenue to add their support for obtaining votes for women in 1920. A friend was ordered not to march by her Quaker husband, so she obeyed him and didn't. Instead, she rode behind in the Whitney's carriage.

My Whitney years were productive ones. In gratitude to Isabel, I researched the life of Ann Hasseltine Judson, which was published under the title of *Golden Boats From Burma* in 1961. It was dedicated to Isabel's beloved sister, Hasseltine, and my great-aunt Sarah Kate Ticehurst Ashdown, sister of Archie and George Ticehurst who married the twins Nellie and Doom. Auntie Kate was a devoted Strict Ebenezer Baptist, who scared me half out of my wits once when I was a child. She caught me planting a primrose on a Sunday and declared on the spot that I was destined for hell. She must have changed her mind upon reading my book about the famed Baptist missionary's wife, dedicated in part, to her. She wrote, "I have never been so honored in all my long life."

Of Adoniram Judson, himself, Isabel confided that the Hasseltines didn't think much of him having three wives, one after the other. "Gentle retribution that he died aboard ship and was buried alone at sea."

Belle Hayes, Isabel's childhood friend, was delighted that Isabel, too, was equally busy with her painting. She commissioned her, as she had in the past, this time to paint a bell-flower ornamental mural for the French chateau-like house she was building in Montecito, near Santa Barbara, California. She also completed a series of watercolors of nature scenes at the Mohonk Mountain House, near New Paltz, New York. We worked so well in the same house. As Marion Foster said one day, "You complement each other."

There was also a deep understanding of the other's needs. Isabel had been disabled at the height of her fame as a fresco painter. No longer able to climb ladders, she had further developed her skills as a watercolorist. I arranged an exhibit of Taos Indian paintings she had done while visiting Mabel Dodge Luhan, American art patron, and her Indian husband, Tony, in Taos, for the Towner Art Gallery, in Eastbourne, England. The gallery was close to Pamela and my school in Eastbourne. We used to visit it during rainy lunch hours. This I did while confined to the house with my old enemy, recurrent bleedings. For months I couldn't even go to the movies, for I never knew when "accidents" were going to happen.

I always associate Isabel with Thanksgiving. That was *our* day. The staff were told to stay home while we went to the National Republican Club for our turkey dinner. Then it was back to Isabel's drawing room to sit on the "Mary and Her Little Lamb" sofa in front of a blazing fire and enjoy Hasseltine's precious collections of portrait miniatures, jewelled watches and scent bottles. Their father's large gold watch had a chain plaited from her mother's long hair.

I discovered that Isabel's health was failing in an odd sort of way. From time to time she restored works of art—another of her gifts—for close friends and the Brooklyn Museum of which her grandfather had been one of the first patrons. She had decided that my family statue of Saint Teresa of Avila needed "to be put into condition." However, when Saint Teresa returned to the fourth floor suite she had acquired one blue eye and one brown eye. Something was wrong, for Isabel was meticulous about such things. Finally, our doctor told me that she would need to curtail her activities and not exhaust herself. I asked if I should cancel the short holiday I had planned in Natchez, New Orleans, and Charleston. "Definitely not," he said. "That would only alarm her." I was 24 when I travelled to the Deep South for the first time, in 1961. I kept thinking how hard it would be for Isabel if she could no longer venture outside, particularly in the winter, to paint her watercolors from nature.

Arriving in the "Holy City," as natives call their Charleston, I was intrigued with its unique tall houses and private walled gardens. The idea came to me that in Charleston's mild climate and a house with a sheltered garden, Isabel could spend the colder months outside with her easel while I wrote indoors. The Christian Herald Family Bookshelf had bought the book club rights to *Golden Boats From Burma*, so I had money to invest. Why not buy us a winter home?

I have always been interested in saving the past, so I was drawn to the excellent work being done by the Historic Charleston Foundation in reclaiming the rundown Ansonborough area, and I wandered around looking at the properties they had for sale. That was how I found the Dr. Joseph Johnson House, built in 1838, and named for its builder, a

Unionist/physician/historian, who had written *Traditions and Reminiscences of the American Revolution, Chiefly in the South.*

With stucco over brick it reminded me of a small fortress; inside, the large rooms were just the kind that Isabel liked. Even hung with cobwebs and falling bits of plaster they were crying out to be saved. Through my British eyes they were majestic. I wasn't a bit dismayed when I saw the room that would eventually be my bedroom, half filled with hay! The garden wasn't much better; it was a wreck, reminding me of the description of Vita Sackville-West's Sissinghurst when she saw it for the first time.

A broken down car lay deserted in one corner mixed in with rubbish of all descriptions: broken bicycle parts, an old doghouse with rusted chain and a motley collection of rotting umbrellas and palmetto fronds. The broken garden walls needed urgent repair to ensure our much-loved privacy. There was one redeeming feature, an enormous live oak that spread out its leafy, green branches dripping with silvery Spanish moss. "We can be very happy here," I thought, and in an excited frame of mind returned to New York.

Once home I wrote to the Historic Charleston Foundation regarding the property. As their director, Frances Edmunds, was passing through New York, it was decided that she should call upon me at the Whitney House, which she did. By the time she left, the contract to purchase was signed and the once proud house with that patriarch of a tree would be Isabel's and mine.

In 1960, the veteran actress, Margaret Rutherford, as popular with Americans as she was at home in her native Britain, had arrived in New York with her actor husband, Stringer Davis, to appear in an ill-fated play, *Farewell, Farewell Eugene.* She had read *Me Papoose Sitter* while riding on top of a red London double-decker bus. So intrigued did she become that she rode past her stop to the end of the bus line and finished up alone in the garage for the night. After that nocturnal experience she was determined to play the role of Poor Old Grandmother should the rumored movie be made. Then finding that I lived in New York, she was determined to meet me. Walking hand in hand with

Stringer she rang the doorbell with some trepidation, as she later said, "Like two hopeful travellers at the end of a long journey, an ethereal feeling swept over us."

Isabel knew they were coming to visit. She kept the news from me on purpose.

Margaret Rutherford's description of Isabel and me has survived: "They could both have stepped out of a play, Miss Whitney ageless and gracious with her bluish-gray hair piled upon her head rather like Queen Mary's. It was ironic that she, who in her youth had made national headlines when she had climbed like King Kong to the top of a skyscraper to paint a fresco, should have crippled herself by falling off a kitchen chair! She walked with a light aluminum crutch which she manipulated with the dexterity of a nubile mountain goat.

"The child (Margaret called me "the child" right from the start even though I was 23) was dark-haired, high cheek-boned and frail. Gordon's large brown eyes, inherited from some long-dead Andalusian ancestor, haunted me all through that evening's performance. He sat with a large green and red Amazon parrot named Marilyn on his shoulder who had just been photographed for *Life* magazine."

Stringer was intimidated by Isabel's sterling silver tea balls. "Cannonballs would be the better word," he confessed. "I was afraid of cracking the cup."

Important visitors always autographed a bookshelf in my library, and while Margaret was adding her signature she exclaimed like a little girl discovering a new secret, "Oh, the Archbishop of Canterbury, Dr. Geoffrey Francis Fisher!" She clapped her hands and began to hum William Blakes *Jerusalem*. Then she found Joan Crawford's name and she clapped her hands again. "My favorite American actress. She invented the wide shoulder look. Ah, in *Mildred Pierce* how she baked those cakes and fought for that ungrateful daughter. Such mother love!"

Then Isabel politely asked Margaret if there was anything she would like to do during her stay in America. "I would like to have Thanksgiving," was the prompt reply.

Isabel then asked if they would like to see the Botticelli. Again, Margaret clapped her hands for joy. "I have always wanted to see a real

Botticelli angel," she said.

"Then you shall see three," replied Isabel, leading the way down the winding staircase.

I quote from my biography, *Margaret Rutherford: A Blithe Spirit:* "As I watched them, I felt a strange longing in my heart, a sense of belonging in a real family, something I had never known. There was something about Margaret Rutherford that was easy to define—compassion, understanding and love. It was all there in her eyes, and when it was time to leave with Stringer, she engulfed me in those ample motherly arms."

Isabel Whitney gave Margaret Rutherford Thanksgiving in July 1960 with turkey and all the trimmings. What I did not know then was that a day or two earlier Margaret and Isabel had met privately to discuss my future, at which the latter had revealed my chronic medical problem. Isabel also revealed that she was in the first stages of leukemia for which her doctor had told her there was no cure. Financially, she would see that I was taken care of. It was the loneliness that she dreaded for me.

A day or so afterwards Margaret and Stringer asked me, while on a visit to the Statue of Liberty, if I would like to join their little family. "We would love to adopt from the heart." I was so happy, for as a British magazine book critic once told me, "Who would not have wanted Margaret Rutherford for his mother?" Isabel was delighted, yet I could not leave her to die alone.

Farewell, Farewell Eugene, which opened September 27, 1960, at The Helen Hayes Theater on Broadway was not a success. The critics hated the play but not my new mother. Walter Kerr, drama critic for the New York *Herald Tribune*, confessed in print that he "had always loved Margaret Rutherford but that by the time she came to America, she had a husband and I had a wife."

I had never called anyone "mother" before. I liked it. Margie was always Margie. That's the way she wanted it. I'd been rejected by my natural father, Jack, with whom I remained estranged for years. In time, I came to think of Stringer as the kind of father I'd always dreamed of.

Mother Rutherford took the play's closing after only seven performances as a personal defeat. Fortunately, dear Danny Kaye had her flown to Hollywood to appear with him, wearing a Scottish tartan sash and a grand bejewelled tiara, in the comedy movie, *On The Double*.

There she met both Clark Gable and Marilyn Monroe who were starring in Arthur Miller's *The Misfits*. Clark planted a big kiss on Mother's forehead, then turned and was gone, turning once under a gaslight prop to wave goodbye.

"We knew he was tired," she later said, "and that he had had a miserable time on the set, but I suddenly got the impression that he was waving as if he were saying goodbye to films, goodbye, in fact, to everything. And of course, soon afterwards the poor man died."

As for Marilyn, Mother called her "that dear waif-child, whom life and Hollywood were destined to destroy. That nice Joe Dimaggio was the only man who loved her truly."

Isabel had good and bad days. Alice Madden, with whom as a girl she had studied in Germany and Russia—Isabel art and Alice singing—invited her to stay in the large white house in Darien, Connecticut. I diplomatically suggested to Alice that Isabel should paint quietly in the garden and not make one of their more strenuous car trips that usually lasted three or four days, driving through New England in search of sketching material for Isabel. Alice readily agreed, but as quickly changed her mind. Two nights later she phoned very upset to tell me that Isabel had collapsed and was in a hospital many miles from New York. When I finally got there Isabel was a mass of tubes, having blood transfusions and crying to go home. The doctor told me that I would take her at my own risk. I hired a private ambulance at once and phoned Marion Foster, who found me a woman doctor who still made house calls, a rarity in New York City. With the help of round-the-clock nurses to help me, Isabel received the kindly home nursing that she needed.

Unfortunately, at times the nurses were more trouble than the patient. It was like running a hospital in the Metropolitan Museum. One nurse in particular was told not to light a fire in one parlor fireplace as the chimney was blocked, but she did anyway, filling the floor with thick black smoke. Fire trucks came from all directions. Strangely,

Isabel loved the commotion. Three days before she died, Isabel's mind was alert and she seemed much better, asking to be wheeled into the drawing room where she trimmed Alice Madden a straw hat with flowers. Then she suddenly said, "Dear Lamb, I don't want to buried in Greenwood with all the others. Aunty Lyd *would* have her two maids buried with her and they were both shaped like pyramids. I would feel so squashed in the middle. I want to be buried with your grandmother in England."

During Cousin Isabel's long illness, throughout 1961 and until her death, two of her most loyal friends, the artists Edward and Jo Hopper, phoned regularly with words of cheer. They lived just around the corner at 3 Washington Square North. I always knew it was them for he spaced his words carefully, while she talked excessively. Like Margie and Jack's, their marriage had not been made in heaven. They quarreled a great deal, with level-headed Isabel often acting as arbitrator. Even she was nonplussed when Jo said she had bitten her husband!

"Why, why did you marry me?" one day Jo asked.

"You have curly hair, you know some French, and you're an orphan," he replied.

Eternally frugal, the Hoppers bought their wardrobes from Sears Roebuck or Woolworth's, wearing them until they were threadbare and patched. When Jo told Isabel that the summer dress she was wearing was 10 years old, Isabel said, "Oh, that's nothing, I'm wearing Mother's dress and she's been gone 29."

I bought two Chihuahuas, Miss Nelly and Miss Annabel-Eliza, to keep me company as Isabel slipped away.

I was with Isabel in the late afternoon on February 2, 1962, when I noticed she had stopped breathing. "Gracie Allen," as we had dubbed her last nurse, for she was so fluttery, was in the kitchen eating her supper. I quietly closed Isabel's eyes, kissed her, then telephoned for Dr. Parks McComb who quickly arrived. Marion Foster came to help me just afterwards.

After a requiem at St. John's in the Village, Isabel's funeral took place at All Saints, Old Heathfield, on St. Valentine's Day 1962, the

Reverend Thomas Savins officiating. The local undertaker, Roy Jarvis, was given the instructions from John Hay Whitney, the ambassador, as to how to fold the American flag that had covered the casket of the country's first woman fresco painter. It was presented to me. Among the floral tributes was one signed "Margaret and Stringer" on an enormous heart-shaped greeting card.

Margie presided at tea in Beecholme afterwards where our mannish cousin, Madge Butler, upset her by devouring all but one of the cream buns. There had also been a funeral lunch in New York at the Whitney House where Mother Rutherford told fellow actress Joan Crawford, "Joan, dear, if you must serve Pepsi-Cola, kindly refrain from using the Rockingham teacups." Joan, of course, was then the widow of Alfred Steele, the Pepsi executive.

Isabel left me the Whitney House, many works of art and $2 million.

I stayed on for a time at Beecholme, visiting favorite childhood places, before going to Elm Close, the Rutherford's home, to sleep in what Mother Rutherford called "the children's room" which had nursery rhymes painted all over the walls. At 25, I was a bit old for nursery rhymes, but I loved it just the same.

Elm Close was a gracious house set in a tiny wood with a real fairy snowdrop ring. Mother said that it was because of the fairy ring that they had really bought the house in the 1950s. Bundled up in heavy jackets and shawls, we breakfasted in front of the snowdrop flowers with a sprinkling of real snow covering the lawn.

Inside, the house was quite cozy in spite of its size. There was a large inglenook by the fireplace where she liked to sit, wearing her felt slippers, and read poetry aloud, pausing every so often to poke the coals burning in the grate.

All around was an eclectic array of personal treasures. These had been collected on far-flung Rutherford-Davis travels and were mixed happily with priceless antiques inherited from Stringer's mother, who cast a somewhat disapproving eye from her portrait in an oval gilt frame that was always falling to pieces at the wrong time. Once when the senior Mrs. Davis fell out in the middle of Mother Rutherford's reading

Cathy's immortal death scene from *Wuthering Heights*, she looked at me and said, "Sometimes I think that Tuft's mother does it on purpose!" She called Stringer by his pet name, "Tuft."

I was cheered by visits with Margie at Beecholme and Mother Rutherford at Elm Close, so I soon felt up to returning to the Whitney House. There I found that the Tiffany window had been stolen. The window was later recovered from an antique shop in Greenwich Village that belonged to the girlfriend of Isabel's former butler.

It took me three weeks to go through the contents of the library. Some antiquarian books I gave to the Library of Congress.

I decided to go forward with the restoration of the house in Charleston. By September it was ready for occupancy.

Blood Sports

*"We do not ask that fate shall
mitigate whatever hardship we
may have to bear."*

John Jarmain

I was driven down to Charleston by friends, arriving September 2, 1962. Just as we approached the Holy City a red cardinal flew into the vehicle, smashed itself against the rear window and spattered me with blood. The driver, more superstitious than the others, called it a bad omen.

As the two truckloads of furniture from the Whitney House were not being unloaded until the next day, I spent my first night with the two Chihuahuas alone in the mansion. My neighbor Landine Manigault, wife of the publisher of the Charleston newspaper, lent me a rubber mattress and two pillows. She was a vibrant person, full of enthusiasm and laughter. Standing in the street in front of 56 Society Street, she shouted up her welcome to me as I stood on the second story piazza.

It was a beautiful restoration that Read Barnes, the architect, had given me. The lower drawing room with its gray-green walls had almost an ethereal glow. The early Empire style mantel that Isabel and I had brought back to its original beauty in New York was now the focal point in the newly refurbished room. Here, the Whitney's 18th century

French commodes would go, and the writing table that had once been Aunt Gertrude Hall's, which I had purchased from a cousin.

In the lower foyer would hang one of a pair of large silver sanctuary lamps from a Persian mosque. Across the foyer in the dining room, painted a rich salmon color, was a pine mantel that came from Salem, Massachusetts, on which the bell-flower carvings were particularly good. This room would be furnished with Queen Anne and Georgian pieces, both British and American, and a pair of mirrors once owned by George Washington. The President had ordered two identical pairs from England, one of which he gave to Isabel's ancestors. The mirrors were coveted for the White House, when First Lady Jacqueline Kennedy sought furniture and art objects with presidential associations during her admirable restoration.

Upstairs on the second floor was the upper drawing room with walls of pale daffodil yellow and an elaborate period pine mantel with Wedgewood plaques that had been imported from Mother Rutherford's own Buckinghamshire. Most of the furnishings would be American Federal, presided over by Rembrandt Peale's portrait of the heroine of my *Golden Boats From Burma*, Ann Hasseltine Judson. Nearby, I would place the beautiful portrait miniature of the Condesa, my great-great-grandmother, with the rich hazel eyes that all her descendants were to inherit.

Opposite was the antebellum bedroom with a floral dogwood wallpaper designed by Isabel. The four-poster bed and the dressing table for this room were both of New Orleans origin, the latter having belonged to Cousin Hasseltine Whitney. The triple decker bed steps were Robert E. Lee's, as were the two bedroom chairs, having come from his former mansion in Arlington, Virginia. Throughout the house I would display fine examples of my silkwork embroidery collection with a most unusual framed scene showing a pheasant standing by a sheath of wheat as the centerpiece. It was of American origin, very valuable. I still have it.

The third floor was inviolate. It was mine. Here was the library-study where I would work. It commanded a view of the old Charleston High School columns in the front, while in the rear it looked out at the giant live oak in the garden. Almost like living in a tree house. Here on the top floor and within my walled garden, I thought I could live with my secret. I was wrong.

That first night was a horror. Seeing the lights go on in Isabel's chandeliers, a group of boisterous sailors, thinking that perchance a bordello had opened, banged on the giant eagle knocker, then climbed over the high wrought iron gates and dropped half drunk into the driveway. Thank goodness the telephone was already turned on. I called for the police, who got rid of the intruders.

Ansonborough, I learned, was not then the genteel neighborhood of today. In those early days one felt rather like a pioneer. One hundred and fifty-five thousand dollars had been spent on the restoration alone, without even counting the garden. That was a lot of money in 1962.

The garden posed a problem. With the exception of the marvelous oak, a broken fragment of red wall with an iron grill on a window that reminded me of Sissinghurst and an avenue of straggly Roses of Sharon that badly needed pruning, nothing remained. It was suggested I engage Loutrel W. Briggs, the dean of Charleston garden designers, to work his own special magic. We were not too compatible. Having been reared in the formal and sedate garden at Sissinghurst, my aesthetic tastes did not run parallel to Loutrel Briggs, who had a penchant for placing in gardens many little cherubs of uncertain sex.

Then there was the tenant in the old kitchen house. She had a large female German shepherd, named Cordelia, who took a violent dislike to poor Mr. Briggs in his neat gray tweeds complete with British gamekeeper hat. One morning, without prior warning, Cordelia charged at the innocent intruder, holding him firm by the seat of his pants. Mr. Briggs was highly indignant. He never returned. Only the driveway design was his.

In desperation, I sent Vita Sackville-West an outline of the unrestored garden which was later redone to her specifications. A garden should be a series of outdoor rooms, opening from one into another. This was successfully achieved in three main sections or outdoor rooms, with a corner backing on to the grilled wall boasting a miniature white garden in honor of the larger, famed one Vita had created at Sissinghurst. In Charleston we used white azaleas, Easter lilies, and then for the hot summer months, silver, cool-looking caladiums. I chose a gray granite Chinese goddess shimmering in white rather than the prissy little cherubs suggested by Mr. Briggs.

As my primary interest in life was writing, I engaged a staff of four to run the house, explaining to all of them that I had an important book set in the Lincoln era to do for my publisher, and that in order to achieve this and to pay their salaries I needed peace. It wasn't that I couldn't afford them. I thought it would give them added incentive if they felt an important part of the picture. Unknown to them, in my physical condition, I quite thought I would be alone for the rest of my life. Marriage was out of the question. My literary dreamworld was its substitute.

A statuesque black woman of 40, Irene, was hired as cook/housekeeper, with a salary that by New York standards was a fair one. When I asked for her Social Security number so that I could make the appropriate deductions, she looked at me with surprise, obviously ignorant of what I was saying. She explained that in her last place of employment she had earned a fraction of what I was prepared to pay her, but as compensation had been allowed to take home all the leftovers.

I explained to Irene that she would have to get a Social Security number before I could legally employ her, then took her myself to the Social Security office in the Federal Building on Meeting Street. Through the grapevine—and in Charleston the house servants heard everything—I soon found that several ladies from old Charleston families thought my paying Irene's Social Security was creating "a dangerous precedent."

Irene's daughter, Mary Ann, wanted to work with her mother, which was soon arranged. The new housekeeper then announced that they both needed uniforms in keeping "with this beautiful house." This was agreed to, but when Irene appeared looking like a hospital nurse with a cap peaked like a crown, it was hard not to smile.

James Fickling, or "Mr. James" as he preferred to be called, came from a long line of Charleston butlers, having just lost his employer through death. Mr. James was a law unto himself. He would wind all the clocks, including the two grandfathers, daring all of us even to touch them. For his daytime chores he wore khaki pants, polished boots, a spotless white shirt and a green baize apron. His more formal attire was a black alpaca jacket or a white linen one, according to the season. He presided over the dining room where his heavy gold watch chain swung like a pendulum, which I was always fearful would upset the soup. As he had known one guest in particular since the man was a small boy, Mr. James was not above telling him, "Finish your rice." He drove a highly polished car of uncertain vintage in which after one grim experience I vowed never to ride. Mr. James was so busy explaining who lived in each house, he often found himself on the wrong side of the street.

At times Irene was as unpredictable as Mr. James. Once, and only once, did I offer to go to the Old City Market for fresh fruit because she would go too. Armed with Uncle Joseph Whitney's silver knobbed cane she cleared me a path through the startled vendors. Scarlett O'Hara never had it so good! I thought we would both be arrested for harassment.

Augustus Lewis, better known as "Gussie," was Mr. James's handpicked choice for under-butler, "Because his Mama is dying the Lord wants you to hire him." Mr. James was an elder in Gussie's church so I had no reason to doubt him. Gussie came early before high school to walk Jacqueline, the new German shepherd puppy, whose mother had so belittled poor Mr. Briggs. The staff were soon calling her Miss Jackie.

Gussie, whom Mr. James cautioned, "You know too much for your age," had a cheerful disposition and was extremely popular. He knew just who was sleeping "with that lady's husband." It used to embarrass me at times, for I had to meet these wandering husbands after church at St. Philip's.

Not since my childhood in England had I enjoyed Christmas so much as I did that first one in Charleston. Landine Manigault brought me a huge bunch of greenery and a large sprig of mistletoe from her mother's plantation at Medway. I don't know whom she thought I would kiss!

Isabel had saved Christmas decorations for years and her mother before her, so we had a unique collection to work with. Gussie was in his element. The mantels looked particularly festive while the Christmas tree was planted in a large flower pot. Mr. James dug it up on his own land on Edisto as he, like me, had a great reverence for trees. After New Year's Day it went right back to Edisto to be planted again.

On Christmas Eve I was writing upstairs when Gussie came rushing in with Miss Jackie barking behind him. "Miss Irene says to come down at once. Mistress Edmunds has sent you a gift."

I followed Gussie down and there lying in state on my Queen Anne dining table was a pheasant, a gay red ribbon tied to its throat.

"Isn't it lovely!" Irene exclaimed. "She brought it herself."

Nodding in reply, I felt slightly uncomfortable at being given this poor dead thing with such glorious plumage. When I suggested that perhaps we should let a taxidermist stuff it, she was horrified. Snatching it up she made straight for the kitchen, which by Mr. James's order was off limits to me.

When the Blake Middletons came to dinner that evening it reappeared, plucked naked all but its head from which its sad eyes still knowingly reproached me.

Charleston society was very nice to me, so I reciprocated by opening my house for the Historic Charleston Foundation's annual tour of homes and gardens. Once I obliged them at a minute's notice when the director's mother was unable to do so because of a death in the family. At such times I stayed in my own domain on the third floor. Although I was entertained at dinner by some prominent families, I did not attend any parties. Except for the occasional glass of champagne or sherry, I don't care for alcohol which goes quickly to my head. I did enjoy private visits to the historic homes, most memorable of which was a visit to the Aiken-Rhett mansion on Elizabeth Street, the home of Frances Dill Rhett. She asked me to identify a large Chinese vase. I picked it up. Then much to my amusement her elderly butler rushed forward to grab it out of my hands. He seemed to be another Mr. James.

Mrs. Rhett's home was a time capsule inside and out, with old carriages still in the stables and even the original outside privies. The great house, c. 1817, had 23 rooms. It was built originally as a single house by John Robinson, a merchant and real estate investor responsible for several houses on neighboring Judith Street. The house later belonged to Gen. William Aiken, who enlarged it several times, finally in the Italianate style.

As Mrs. Rhett led me through a procession of rooms, all filled with furnishings and paintings collected over several generations, her butler followed us a little way behind. She pointed out the "cooling couch" upon which the family had laid out its dead and a locked door shutting off a room which she said had not been opened since she came to the house as a bride. I couldn't help thinking of Charles Dickens's *Great Expectations* with Miss Haversham, an old lady still in her wedding gown, the house festooned with cobwebs and on the table, a molding wedding cake.

Workwise, Charleston was very good to me. Nobody seemed to worry that I didn't go to parties as I was always conveniently there when needed to open my house for spring tours. Preservation and restoration of old houses I had learned as a child from Uncle George Ticehurst, the care of fine furnishings from dear Aunty Doom. When somebody was urgently needed to put up the money and save the old high school opposite my home on Society Street, I bought it. During the city's earthquake of 1886 the terra cotta acanthus leaves that decorated the pillar tops had fallen and were thought lost. Planting a magnolia tree on my newly acquired property, Mr. James and Gussie found them buried in the ground. How I wish Pamela Pike, my archaeologist school friend, had been with us then. She would have loved it.

During those first months on Society Street, I had three biographies under contract while another on two Colorado explorers was commissioned. I liked to be busy. There was no time to brood on my physical condition.

The first book I wrote in Charleston was *Vinnie Ream—The Girl Who Sculptured Lincoln.* I had never heard of the heroine until one day, after visiting Arnold Tovell, then managing editor of Holt, Rinehart and

Winston, the New York publishers, he came flying after me down Madison Avenue flourishing a yellowed newspaper clipping, thrusting it into my hand.

"Write me a book about her," he ordered, then turned and hurried back to his office. I read the story, dated 1929, that told of Vinnie Ream, a young girl who was a protégée of the sculptor Clark Mills, who took her to the White House to meet Abraham Lincoln. At President Lincoln's invitation, Vinnie was allowed to return for a short period each afternoon to sculpt a head of the President from clay. As he had just lost his small son Willie, his face showed the sorrow. Vinnie was working at the White House the day that Lincoln was shot. History had conveniently forgotten the fact, so any book was a challenge.

Later, Vinnie became the first woman commissioned by Congress to do a sculpture. She made the full-length statue of the slain president for the Capitol rotunda. Generations later, millions would see the Lincoln figure, carved from white marble (chosen by Vinnie at the famed Carrara marble works in Italy), as it looked sadly down on the casket of another murdered president, John F. Kennedy.

My research on Vinnie Ream took me to places as diverse as Oshkosh, Wisconsin, Vinnie's birthplace, and the Library of Congress, where I found a cache of her personal papers that included a horrid letter from Mary Todd Lincoln, sent in response to an innocent letter of sympathy. Mrs. Lincoln was a jealous woman. Vinnie was young and beautiful.

Vinne Ream—The Girl Who Sculptured Lincoln, written as a "young adult" book, was published in 1963. The book made history of sorts on Madison Avenue, being selected as the monthly choice of an adult book club where it, in turn, led the bestseller list for seven months, enabling me to buy an oil painting by Washington Allston that now hangs in the Museum of Early Southern Decorative Arts in Winston-Salem, North Carolina.

Thanks to Charleston bookseller Edwin Peacock, I met Carson McCullers who was visiting him. I met the author of such novels as *The Heart is a Lonely Hunter*, *The Member of the Wedding* and *Reflections in a*

Golden Eye in a Mt. Pleasant garden filled with white wisteria. She greeted me with the disarming words, "You're really a little girl." Having been crippled at an early age by a stroke, she was acutely aware of others' disabilities. The small, bird-like writer became good friends with me. I often visited at her home in Nyack, New York, where she always served champagne, except when actress Helen Hayes, a neighbor who preferred tea, came to visit. When Carson went out in the evening, she often returned to find her long-time friend, playwright Tennessee Williams, sitting on the doorstep with all of his problems to solve. He was a very lonely man when his confidante, Carson, passed away September 29, 1967. Williams was to have narrated Dena Crane's video on my life, but died suddenly in February 1983 before he could do it.

Middle-aged Durant Macrae, the Macrae Smith Company publisher, had been introduced to me by Margaret Campbell Barnes, the Isle of Wight author who had published several highly successful historical novels including *My Lady of Cleves* (about the much-wed Henry VIII's sensible fourth wife). One day he confided to me that he wished somebody would write a book for him on one of his family's acquaintances, Baby Doe Tabor, popularly known as the Silver Queen of Colorado, on account of her husband's silver mine. Could I oblige him with that book? Well I have never refused a challenge and, as Mother Rutherford often said, most of our best contacts are made over the garden fence. I accepted, although at the time I knew nothing of Colorado history except what I had seen in Hollywood westerns.

Vita Sackville-West was much interested when Margie told her of my latest writing project. When told that President Chester B. Arthur had been a guest at Baby Doe's wedding, March 1, 1883, Vita immediately sent me a note to say how that same American president had once proposed marriage to her mother, then Victoria West, the toast of Washington society. The illegitimate daughter of Lionel Sackville-West through his liason with Pepita, a Spanish dancer, Miss Victoria West was his official hostess at the British Legation in Washington. Her great beauty attracted many men. She later wed her cousin, another Lionel, later Lord Sackville, and became Lady Sackville.

Emeline K. Paige, editor of *The Villager*, put me in touch with

Ninita Bristowe Reis, an ever-young lady with Colorado connections who lived in the old Grosvenor Hotel on New York's lower Fifth Avenue. She, in turn, gave me a letter of introduction to a former lady explorer, Verona (call me "Brownie") Adams, which I carried hopefully to Denver. Mrs. Adams responded graciously by giving a tea for me at her home, Vagabond House, which stood in a magnificent garden. There I was seated in the middle of a circle of well-preserved older ladies wearing the most jewels I've seen since visiting the Tower of London. They all talked at once about everything but Baby Doe. In dismay, I returned empty handed to the Brown Palace Hotel.

That evening Brownie Adams called to say that she and her friends had been impressed by my "combined modesty and frailty," whatever that might mean, and were all ready to help. They did. Trips were arranged for me to visit museums, libraries and private collections. I was taken up the mountain road to Leadville, Colorado, where Baby Doe, widowed and alone, had been found frozen to death in 1935, still guarding her late husband Horace Tabor's Matchless Mine. He had told her never to desert it, and she never did.

In 1962, Durant Macrae was delighted to publish the result of my efforts, entitled *The Two Lives of Baby Doe*, about her prime as the Silver Queen of Colorado and her life after as an elderly recluse.

My friendship with Brownie Adams continued. One morning she phoned me in Charleston to inform me that I should be her late husband Roy's biographer, that she had booked a first class flight for me to Denver the following week, and that I would be given a suite at the Brown Palace. She would pay me $50,000. *I was in shock.*

Flying out to Denver I wondered why I had accepted such a task. Perhaps it was because wealthy Brownie Adams had never in her life been refused. Her husband, a relative of Jack London whom he never acknowledged, thinking his novels too coarse, had indulged all her whims. Their home was an example, crammed full of "treasures" from San Francisco's Chinatown and mementoes of the countries they had visited. She handed me scrapbooks filled with photographs they had taken in Africa, the Middle East and China during the 1920s. They wore pith helmets and neat khaki outfits by day. And, wherever their tent was pitched—in the jungle or the desert—they always dressed in evening clothes for dinner. As Mother would have said somewhat charitably, "They have stepped right out of Noel Coward."

To make these materials palatable to the average reader was one thing; to find a publisher was another. One morning, without any prior warning and while I was still laboring over the manuscript I was writing for her, Brownie phoned again. "I have engaged the Grand Ball Room at the Brown Palace to launch Dear Vagabonds," as she had decided it was to be called. "I have invited the Governor of Colorado and he has accepted."

"But, Brownie, the book isn't quite finished and we still have to find a publisher."

"I leave all that to you, and if you have to pay to get it in print, money as you know, is no object."

Then I thought of my grandmother's old newspaper put out by the reputable Southern Publishing Company in Brighton, England, who in turn came to my rescue. For a most reasonable sum they published the book with excellent reproductions of the Adams's treasured photographs. Brownie's favorite symbol of two serpents even graced the cover.

For the Governor's visit Brownie Adams moved me, Mr. James in his best church-going suit, Annabel-Eliza and Nelly, the two Chihuahuas, and Miss Jackie, rapidly growing into a large German shepherd, lock, stock and barrel, dog food included, to the renowned Brown Palace Hotel in Denver.

Mr. James's official capacity, Brownie said, was to look after the dogs, who in due course were to meet the startled governor. Miss Jackie arrived wearing a collar Mr. James had made out of Isabel's best pearls. Mr. James, however, was not intimidated by Denver at all. He grumbled how the women were "too skinny and sassy."

So Brownie had her book, published in 1963. She was delighted and grateful. Three days before she died on March 18, 1968, she phoned from the hospital to thank me again. In her will she left me $10,000.

I now had to finish *Mr. Jefferson's Ladies*, a low-key biography I was writing for Holt, Rinehart and Winston. Dedicated to Vita Sackville-West and her husband, Harold Nicolson, it traced the lives of Thomas Jefferson's wife, Martha Wayles Jefferson, who died young, and of their daughters, Martha (Patsy) and Mary (Maria). As I wanted to capture the feel of Monticello, the fabled Jefferson home in Virginia, I visited it early one morning without benefit of tourists. There wasn't a single footstep in the sprinkling of snow that covered the driveway. The feeling was eerie, like stepping back in time.

Sadly, Vita never knew of the joint dedication as she died of cancer at Sissinghurst, June 2, 1962. After a funeral service in Holy Trinity, Sissinghurst, her body was cremated at Charing. The ashes were placed in the small marble sarcophagus which had once housed her inkwells, then taken to St. Michael and All Angels at Withyham to lie among the Sackvilles in their own family crypt. Writing somewhat critically from Sissinghurst, Margie tartly commented, "She has left Jack (Copper) a brace of pistols. Maybe she thought he would shoot himself."

Meanwhile at Gerrard's Cross, the village in which Elm Close was located, life was busier than it ever had been. Christmas morning 1960, Mother Rutherford had telephoned the movie director, George Pollock, to announce, "This is Miss Rutherford speaking. I would be honored to play Miss Jane Marple." With the Miss Marple roles, Mother Rutherford's movie career had taken a turn for the better. She soon became MGM's most highly paid actress. She now had lots of money to spend on antiques, and spend she did until the tax man again stepped in.

Mother Rutherford's robust portrayal of Agatha Christie's woman detective became a series of four successful movies for MGM that were fun to make and financially rewarding. Fellow actor Robert Morley recalls that Margaret and Stringer were divinely happy together. Morley said, "On country walks together he was reported to pluck bouquets from the hedgerows and present them to her on his knees which must have got rather muddy."

It was quite true. Father was very theatrical.

During the glory days of the astronauts, Mother played the movies'

Grand Duchess Gloriana XIII in the space-race spoof, *Mouse on the Moon*. She was then flown to Cape Canaveral to promote it. Bedridden temporarily with an "issue of blood," I was too weak to go. But from New York, she wrote:

> Dearest Child:
> It was most frustrating flying over what surely must have been your home in Charleston. If I could, I would have parachuted down to see you.
> Mother

Mother's next foray in film was to play the Duchess of Brighton, "A woman," as she said, "of substance and integrity." The cast was led by those star-crossed lovers, Elizabeth Taylor and Richard Burton, both of whom she admired very much. Mother's best remembered line is when she called the flight attendant "conductress," as if she were still riding on a double-decker bus. Of Elizabeth and Richard she said: "It's no secret that they can both act beautifully but at times it became a "who is better?" contest. Elizabeth would play a scene to the very hilt and make it the zenith of perfection. Richard would then come along and try to top it with his own brand of dynamism. They would then ask me to select the winner. This was rather hard, having to choose between my favorite Caesar and Cleopatra."

During the filming I was briefly in England when early one morning, Mother, driving by pony and trap to the movie studios, stopped first to pick a daffodil, the Welsh national emblem. "To give to dear Richard," she explained. "He is so proud to be Welsh."

Mother Rutherford paid a special visit to Old Heathfield, the Sussex village where I was born, to unveil the Anglo American Friendship window that I had given the church in memory of my grandmother and her twin, Aunty Doom. As a child, I remember Uncle Ditcher telling me the story of a former vicar of the parish, the Rev. Robert Hunt, who in 1607, became chaplain to the original Jamestown settlement in Virginia. However, no monument of any kind to record so historic an event then existed in All Saints Parish Church. I vowed that if I ever made enough money one day it should be righted. With the support of the vicar, the Rev. Thomas Savins, a vigorous man with a speaking voice that reminded mother of Laurence Olivier's, I commissioned Laurence Lee to design our memorial. He had been responsible for some of the splendid glass in Coventry Cathedral, replacing that lost in the Second World War bombing. The resulting window showed the Rev. Hunt celebrating the first Anglican communion service on American soil. The two Indian children in the window have the faces of my grandmother and her twin as little children, taken from an old photograph on Brighton Beach.

At the dedication, summer of 1964, Mother Rutherford read the lesson from Hebrews 10:13-14, her own choice: "From henceforth expecting till His enemies be made His footstool. For by one offering He hath perfected for ever them that are sanctified."

She was very pleased with Tom Savins's sermon, in which he noted, "all up and down the country are windows commemorating lords and ladies, admirals and generals, but ours is different. It was been given in the memory of two housewives."

The occasion was the continuation of a cherished friendship with the Savins family, including their younger son Philip, an accomplished photographer. (Philip later carried the processional cross at my wedding in Hastings and was named one of Natasha Manigault Simmons's godfathers.)

Three grand Charleston ladies were in London at the time of the window dedication, so we invited them to the service and reception afterwards. For some ungodly reason they saw fit to travel the 50 miles from London by taxi and later back as they had told the only too happy cabbie to wait for them. He charged *me* £213 for their presence!

Six White Horses

*"More beautiful than fact may be
... the shadow on the wall."*
Vita Sackville-West

Returning to my house in Charleston, I was destined soon afterwards to experience the most shocking of nightmares. I dreamed of six white horses with black plumes on their heads leading a Victorian glass hearse with an open, old-fashioned coffin slowly through the gates into Sissinghurst Cemetery. I looked into the coffin and there I lay...with a smile on my face.

"No, no, no!" I screamed out, but my feet were leaden. I couldn't move.

"Yes, yes, yes," came a chorus of voices. There, bright as day, were my Grandmother, Aunty Doom and Cousin Isabel, who was no longer in need of her cane.

"You are free," another voice spoke with a rich Spanish accent. It was the lady in the miniature, my great-great grandmother, the Condesa, a romantic red rose still pinned at her breast. "You are free!"

"No...no...no..." I cried out again as I opened my eyes to the sound of soft padding feet.

"Oh, Lord Jesus," Irene was screaming. "Mr. James! Call for an ambulance!" Mary Ann, the maid, was crying. Gussie gasped as he saw all the blood, then turned and ran downstairs to find the old butler.

I had suffered a bad hemorrhage. In that awful moment I realized that something had to be done to put things right or I would die. I thought of Vita Sackville-West and the hemorrhage she had on the train foretelling her end from stomach cancer.

The ambulance came. I was taken to Roper Hospital, prepared for the worst. I was there several days during which time a gynecologist, Dr. Oliver Williamson, visited me. "I think you already know what I am going to tell you. I know and you know that for years you have been living out a lie. The blood...it was menstrual."

Dr. Williamson reminded me that the British are noted for keeping a stiff upper lip. He also told me that I couldn't change the way God made me.

My special nurse was Mary Kaye Hardee, a devoted Catholic who helped me so kindly in those first days as Dawn. Impatient to get on with the life I was born to lead, I changed my name at once to Dawn, for the dawn of a new day, followed by Pepita in honor of Vita Sackville-West, whose most popular biography had told of Pepita, her Spanish gypsy grandmother. How Vita would have relished all this: she, Virginia Woolf's fictional Orlando, who over the years had turned from a handsome youth into a beautiful woman and me, the child whose first writings she had so proudly read in her writing room in the tower at Sissinghurst, destined to be the real thing.

I called Mother Rutherford with the news immediately. To which she exclaimed, "I have always wanted another daughter. I shall call you Pepita." And she did.

Dear Margie wrote, "We are both vindicated. Now if only people will be kind there may yet be peace." For some reason she did not tell Jack, who didn't find out about his new daughter until he read it in the *News of the World*. In 1968, my story was news.

However, I wasn't quite out of the woods. Some surgery was needed to open a partially closed vagina, as Wendy Cooper reported in the London *Daily Telegraph*.

As I believe in second opinions, I did see another gynecologist, Dr. Elliot Phipps, of London, who only confirmed what the first had said, if anything even more forcibly. "You are, and always have been, a woman."

He then handed me a paper written by Dr. James F. Glenn, Chief of Urology at Duke University. The paper read: "Parents of children born with genital defects should not waste a day in having tests done that will lead to the establishment of the child's most suitable sex identity. The diagnosis and the decision of whether the child should be male or female can be made as early as the first week of life. The younger the better, to prevent the many psychological problems that can arise."

I accepted Dr. Phipps' word as the final one, and began to make the necessary changes.

It was Father Stringer, who saw goodness in everything, who really had the final word. He cautioned me, "Never look down on Gordon, who over the years was very brave."

I would have preferred to retire gracefully for the next few months, to quietly reflect on the future in the privacy of my Charleston home and garden. First, however, there were two commitments to fulfill: one a personal appearance in Nevada, Missouri, to raise funds for the Bushwacker Museum; the other to make several trips to the White House for a book I was doing on the new First Lady, Lady Bird Johnson. As my body was already undergoing noticeable changes, neither were easy. My breasts were growing, even though I thought it unhealthy to take hormones and discontinued hormone therapy after only three days.

How I got through my talk in Nevada, I will never know. I felt terribly self-conscious in my condition; and as former society editor of the local *Nevada Daily Mail*, I kept running into former colleagues.

I found the Johnson White House brimming with Texas hospitality. Upon arrival, Liz Carpenter, Mrs. Johnson's right hand, made sure there were cookies and coffee. As for Mrs. Johnson, with our mutual love of trees and wildflowers, I found her very responsive and easy to write about.

Then there was my Richard-Rufus!

Richard-Rufus was an elderly black Chihuahua whose acquaintance I first made at the vet's while taking Miss Jackie for her shots. There he sat forlornly in a large old-fashioned parrot cage.

"Who is that?" I asked. "Is he sick? He looks so sad."

"He's fine, just old," said the vet. "His owner brought him in to be put to sleep. I would like to put *her* to sleep."

I looked at Richard-Rufus and he looked at me.

"Could I have him?" I asked.

"Well," said the vet, "I'll go in the back and that way I'll not know from anything what you two do." He conveniently unlatched the cage, then disappeared. I picked up Richard-Rufus, who did not resist, and took him home with Miss Jackie.

For the next three days the old Chihuahua refused to leave me or to take food from anyone else, much to the disgust of Gussie who was devoted to my pets. When Mrs. Carpenter phoned to say I was to be at the White House at ten o'clock the next morning I had to tell her, "I'm sorry, but I cannot leave Richard-Rufus."

"Who is Richard-Rufus?" a somewhat surprised Mrs. Carpenter asked, so I told her his story.

"Hold on, while I speak to Mrs. Johnson."

"We like dogs," Mrs. Carpenter said when she got back on the phone. "Mrs. Johnson says you are to bring Richard-Rufus to the White House."

So the little unwanted Chihuahua, whose only crime was being old, less than a week after he was supposed to be officially dead, flew to the executive mansion where Lyndon B. Johnson dangled him lovingly on his presidential knee.

As a footnote, Mrs. Johnson liked what she read, buying thirty copies of *Lady Bird and Her Daughters*. She never knew with what fear and trepidation I made those visits to the White House. On the final occasion my suit jacket refused to hang properly because of my fast swelling breasts. I felt sure the White House guards were eyeing me suspiciously.

To some it might all seem very romantic turning into a modern Orlando, but in the late 1960s things had to be done legally. First, there was the official change of Christian names handled by my attorney. The

State Department later changed my name on my naturalization papers. Then, I was baptized Dawn Pepita Langley at the AME Church on Smith Street, Shiloh as I called it, as a blessing of my new life. A personal letter was sent to relatives and close friends.

Elsie Knight, my old Sunday school teacher to whom I had just given the gift of a vacation in Holland, responded by mailing me a card with a windmill on the front, and a message that read: "The Lord be praised! He and I knew it all the time!"

In my personal letter I explained how I had envied my sister Fay and Burgess cousins, Peter, Patricia and Sally, their children; how all through the years I had longed for a family of my own; that because of a freak of nature and an ignorant midwife, such fulfillment had long been denied me.

Unfortunately, none of those close female relatives were on hand to help me choose a new wardrobe. Mercifully, I was guided by Rosalie Meyers, who had a dress shop on King Street called Bridals. She had a private room at the back where I conducted my business. I went alone as I had no female relative to shop for me, as Dr. Williamson had suggested. Rosalie, who was very motherly, picked out the underclothing and taught me sizes. Gwen Robyns would later introduce me to pantyhose. I practiced with high heels. My friend Richia Atkinson Barloga was a great help. Her mother, Josephine Atkinson, of Shreveport, Louisiana, sent me beautiful clothes. Marion Foster, Isabel's friend, sent me a lovely pair of yellow shoes from New York.

When I informed my staff that they now had a mistress instead of a master there was a moment of deep silence, then Mr. James suddenly shouted, "Alleluia, Jesus. We have our own miracle."

"Amen," chorused Irene, Mary and Gussie.

J.P. Donleavy, author of the best seller, *The Ginger Man*, once said that "Isolation is part of being an author." It was then no real hardship when I voluntarily incarcerated myself at the mansion while the so-called change was going on, and while awaiting the minor surgery needed to complete it.

I suppose the word change was first spoken to me by the doctors. I have always hated the term "sex change," which is used by the press in a sensational manner, lumping all sorts of changes together. Remember, I had no choice and what was going on inside of me could have caused my death in time, so Dr. Bill McAleenan, my doctor in Eastbourne, England, insisted. I had no choice.

The surgery, to remove deformed flesh around the clitoris, was performed at Johns Hopkins Hospital in Baltimore, Maryland, in September 1968.

It was a medical thing, and in the beginning was treated as such in Charleston and by my family. It was embarrassing to some, a tragedy to others, and to some, it was something that simply should have been taken care of earlier.

I had a friend in Hudson, New York, whose daughter was born the same way, but the problem was corrected at birth.

Still, my story was news and the number one topic on the local cocktail circuit, but Charleston society had survived worse scandals. In time, I thought, everyone would get over it.

My staff and friends did, by degrees. My staff were not critical of me in a dress, although the cook said she needed to fatten me up a bit as only no good men like skinny women.

West Grant, a local hairdresser, took charge of my hair and make-up. My hair grew quickly, and I adopted Margie's shoulder-length style.

My brown hair that for years I had worn cropped close to my head ("Like a convict," Margie grumbled), grew like a weed with one large wave to the side like that from an old portrait I had inherited from my young grandfather, Archibald Ticehurst. For a time I wore colorful slacks before changing to dresses and skirts. I never, on principle, wore pants again.

All in all, the transition took three months. I made good use of the time by doing the vast, time-consuming research needed to write the biography *William, Father of the Netherlands* for Rand McNally. Margie had once said that I was not to dedicate a book to her unless it was the biography of a personage from European history. Up until then my biographies had all been American. She liked the idea of my writing about William because, she said, "He must have been a great dog lover to have his pet hound's effigy carved on his tomb."

News travels fast in the Holy City and as one prominent Charlestonian once told me, "What one doesn't know one makes up." There were smiles, whispers and snickers. But these were offset by virtue of my prominence as a moneyed author with a house full of antiques and art treasures. "And all that money," as one lady on Tradd Street so sagely observed. "And she is eligible," said another on Church Street.

Gussie, who was very popular with a married gentleman on East Bay Street (I could never think why he didn't just go and work for him; he spent enough of my time there), reported there was eager speculation as to whom I might marry. One of my favorite Charleston men Andrew Simons (We both loved photography) and his aunt, Sara Hastie, often invited me to her Roper House mansion, where in 1990 Prince Charles would stay. She showed me slides that Andrew had made. One in particular still stands out in my mind: Andrew riding a camel in front of the pyramids. I hadn't seen him in months, but venturing out one evening to a supermarket with Mr. James, his grocery cart collided with mine. Knowing of the gossip, I guess I turned crimson. "I hear we're getting married," he said, breaking the ice. "When is the wedding?" He was such a dear man. We both had a good laugh. He died shortly thereafter. I still put a red rose on his grave in St. Andrew's Episcopal churchyard when I visit Charleston.

I spent some time at the Women's Clinic at Johns Hopkins in Baltimore to prepare for my new role as a woman. The doctors were surprised by my high IQ. "And yet," said one psychiatrist, "in the subject of men she has the mind of a 14-year old girl."

Whither Thou Goest, I Will Go

*"Entreat me not to leave thee, or
to return from following after
thee: for whither thou goest, I
will go; and where thou lodgest I
will lodge; thy people shall be my
people, and thy God my God."*

Ruth 1:16

I was often reminded of Ruth's immortal words from the Old
Testament on some of the darker days that were to follow. They
always seemed comforting and strangely appropriate.

John-Paul said that he first saw me by the big fountain in Marion
Square. He said the next time he saw me I was dressed all in white,
walking with a man in my garden in the moonlight. He said, "You were
the whitest white woman I had ever seen."

It was a rather mundane beginning to our relationship.

Whenever my cook had a heavy date she gave me frozen fish fingers
for dinner. To this day I hate them. The house had been open for visitors that afternoon. It was September 1968. Mr. James, himself, had
gone courting; it was his night off.

As I sat alone in the candlelit dining room I asked Irene, "Who is
the lucky man?" to which she replied none too pleasantly, "His name is
Simmons, and Simmons is late." As soon as I had finished eating she

gathered up my plate, then left the house in a huff. I was enjoying my coffee when five minutes afterwards the doorbell rang. There stood a broad shouldered black man; apparently, Irene's late date. He was not tall, standing an inch or two higher than me.

Neither of us said a word, then slowly he put out his hand and I did the same. His fingers touched mine, then suddenly he was gone. The darkness swallowed him up.

Next day he telephoned several times asking to speak with me, never giving his name. I was not told of the calls. As Gussie later informed me, Mr. James had told them it "was a black voice...somebody's looking for a job."

That evening I decided to eat informally down in the Stone Room, once the old kitchen. Irene was off, so my supper was brought to me on a tray. Watching the six o'clock news, from the new kitchen above me came the sound of raised voices and the sounds of a scuffle. Suddenly, the door opened and somebody rushed downstairs and tripped. The next thing I knew my supper was on the floor with the air raining wet flowers.

It was a grease covered John-Paul Simmons, still in overalls from the Simmons garage (no relation) where he worked. He had bought me a pail full of flowers from the Old City Market, water and all!

There we sat on the floor dripping calla lilies and Confederate roses with Mr. James, like a dark menacing angel, pointing a shotgun at the visitor's head. It was very Rutherfordish, like a scene from her movies. I started to laugh.

But my visitor was dead serious.

"I will never leave you again," said John-Paul Simmons, and, in his own fashion—for he always came back—he never really did.

I responded to John-Paul's joy of life, his smile, the bunch of wildflowers tucked into his jeans back pocket. He always picked me flowers, just as Father Stringer did for Mother Rutherford. He had a great compassion for animals and old people. He promised to love and care for me. He was determined to have me, and he was brave about it. He fully

68

expected to be lynched after a Society Street neighbor hung a black man in effigy.

It was not an easy courtship, and carried on after darkness. Most local courting couples parked their cars on the Battery, but that was off-limits to us. Like mental telepathy, the police chief, John Conroy, would appear with his flashlight, shine it right in our faces, ordering John-Paul to drive on.

After that I would wait for the sound of his horn, then run downstairs with Miss Jackie at my heels. Away we would drive in the bright red Thunderbird, to the sound of Sam Cooke melodies, over the long Cooper River Bridge to Mount Pleasant. There John-Paul knew a small café bar where the lights were dim, the blues were played and the owner didn't care what my skin color was. He brewed us fresh coffee and left us in peace. When I admired a statue of the Virgin Mary standing in the window, he gave it to us for a gift.

If only the press had left us alone. After John-Paul had asked me to marry him, and I'd accepted, the stories that went out over the Charleston wire services were both cheap and appalling. Much was made of the "fact" that John-Paul was poor and I was rich. Yet, his father, Deacon Joseph Simmons, owned his own home and worked at the Charleston Naval Base. By black standards in that day, he'd done well. When the stories reached England, Mother Rutherford gallantly defended me. Race was not the issue with Father Stringer or her. Her cousin, Tony Benn, was one of the most liberal politicians in the House of Commons. There was no objection there to my marrying a black man, while Margie simply commented, "We are all God's children," and left it at that.

Sometimes Mother's off-the-cuff replies were hilarious. When asked by *Time* magazine if she approved of the courtship, she replied, "Oh, I don't mind Dawn marrying a black man but I do wish she wasn't marrying a Baptist." That quote was picked up by the popular television series "Laugh In."

To me she pronounced an old English proverb, "A man worth lying down with is worth standing up with." She meant it.

A very proper notice of the engagement appeared on the court page of London's *Daily Telegraph*. In common with other ladies of her generation, Mother Rutherford firmly believed that nobody was actually born, married or dead unless it appeared first in that prestigious newspaper.

One afternoon shortly thereafter, three elderly ladies from Charleston society, white gloves, long skirts and all, arrived at my home bearing gifts—an apple pie for me and a watermelon for John-Paul. One asked why I couldn't be like another white lady who fell madly in love with her black butler, but had properly married a white man. For years they all lived in her crumbling mansion, a happy ménage à trois. Then, one of the three women, Mrs. Frances Dill Rhett, made a dire prediction. "If, Miss Hall, you insist on going through with this disastrous union you will end up dead on a cooling couch."

I could have slaughtered John-Paul when I told him all this. He only asked where was his watermelon!

Not content with that foray, another Charleston lady actually turned up on my parents' doorstep at Elm Close begging them to please stop our engagement and wedding.

Mother was furious; she thought of Miss Pross in Dickens' *A Tale of Two Cities*, a role she had always wanted to play. "I am an English woman," she began, but then good manners prevailed and she invited the woman to tea. Father Stringer then gave the lady a stern lecture on slavery in the Seychelles. When they finally got rid of her they gladly paid for her taxi to Gerrard's Cross station.

An engagement photograph was taken. My only copy was mysteriously taken from its silver Art Nouveau frame in the lower drawing room. This was on a Tuesday. On the following Sunday it appeared in the London *News of the World* with headlines screaming: "Royal Biographer To Marry Her Butler."

"What would it matter, if he were a good butler," Mother Rutherford told Princess Margaret when she asked if it were true. "In any case," Mother later told me, "the Queen is sympathetic."

Although my parents were outwardly elated, my doctors at the Women's Clinic in Baltimore were not. The psychiatrists who'd interviewed me demanded I bring John-Paul in to meet them; then they would pass judgement. I let them. I guess I thought that if there was a reason not to marry John-Paul, the so-called experts would tell me. He was interviewed on his own by 16 doctors, charming them all. "We think you are a wonderful young couple," the word later came from their spokesman, "but you will probably be murdered." I was 30 years old. John-Paul was 20.

We immediately left Baltimore for Washington where I opened an exhibition of Isabel's watercolors, making the front page of one of the tabloids. At the hotel the concierge made me smile when he exclaimed in all sincerity, "Madam, I didn't realize you were marrying an African diplomat!" It must have been John-Paul's long black cape that made him look so regal.

However, later in New York where we were met by his mother, who was there visiting relatives, things were not so rosy. After an engagement party at the home of literary agent Jay Garon, graced by actress Hedy Lamarr, who was shown on the late news with me in a backless white crepe de chine gown, we visited some of his family members in Brooklyn. Back at the St. George Hotel where I had stayed many times before, John-Paul suddenly went berserk, flailing about with his hands. His mother wisely stepped out of the way while I got hit so hard that an earring was literally torn out of my ear. He then kicked me on the leg hard enough to draw blood. It was all very embarrassing, with a bellhop scurrying for a first aid box. Another led my fiancé up to his bed. Next morning, his mother, suggested we go ahead and catch the plane back to Charleston without him. She was furious with him. I was confused. But, I couldn't leave him. He went with us, though no one spoke to him on the trip.

I was now having doubts about going through with the wedding, especially as John-Paul's doctor thought he might have had some kind of epileptic seizure. John-Paul didn't remember what happened in New York. Very upset, I slipped away without telling anyone where I was going. I flew to Dr. Raymond Smith's home in Atlantic City, New Jersey. Raymond, a dear friend of Isabel's and mine, and always the gentleman, was sweet. I also sought his advice because he was black and I thought he'd be fair to John-Paul. His advice was to postpone the wedding.

I was tempted to stay on at his home, out of the spotlight, and would have done so if we had not had the most stupid of tiffs. He had read in some newspaper that I was seven years younger than he thought, and I tried to explain that in order to find work on the Winnipeg *Free Press*, which I had desperately needed, having been stranded in Canada, that I had put up my age in order to survive.

Raymond took me to the airport, me in a large black picture hat covered with red poppies. This time, he kissed me goodbye. Although we later spoke many times on the phone, I never saw him again.

Back at home that night, John-Paul crawled through the window, waking me, and ordered, "Get the license. We are being married tomorrow."

I melted.

I informed my family right away. In England, my Burgess cousins and cousin Tony Benn were loyal and kind, and, of course, Aunty Babs. My good friend of the Whitney days, movie queen Joan Crawford, spoke up for me. "The heart knows why," she told Mother Rutherford, and sent me a huge bouquet of yellow rose buds together with a yellow ribbon for Miss Jackie to wear. Miss Crawford liked dogs.

Contrary to local rumor, none of my dogs participated in my wedding. They hid upstairs under my bed.

Helen Hayes, whom I had met for tea at Carson McCullers' home in Nyack, New York, wrote me a letter of encouragement as she had when I was only 20 and had just written "the first interracial morality play," *Saraband for a Saint*. "There is no racial or religious prejudice among people in the theater," Miss Hayes insisted. "The only prejudice is against bad actors, especially successful ones."

Laurence Olivier a friend of Mother Rutherford's advised "Remain true to your ideals." Miss Hayes wrote, "Remember Othello."

Looking back, I think that my parents viewed John-Paul rather theatrically like a latter-day Othello, or as the kind of modern African leader that the Tony Benns were fond of entertaining. "Maybe John-Paul will look like some exotic African chieftain, or even Sidney Poitier," Mother kept telling Father Stringer. Later, after meeting him for the first time and being asked by a lady journalist what she thought of her future son-in-law, she thought carefully for a moment, then replied, "Well, he does have a nice neck!" On one thing she was adamant. "No wedding march for you," she declared when told we would probably be married in Charleston. "I want 'The Battle Hymn of the Republic.' "

The Wedding That Rocked
Charleston Society

"No path of flowers leads to glory."
Jean de la Fontaine

T he problem was to find somebody brave enough to marry us. The
legal requirements had been met when the medical personnel at
Roper Hospital confirmed that I had always been a woman. Now all we
needed was a minister. I attended St. Philip's, but the pastor there wrig-
gled out of conducting the service by suggesting I wait for someone better suited to my station in life. John-Paul's family minster seemed the
logical choice, so I called on him.

I had never seen such a splendid minister's office, filled with all the
latest in furnishings and equipment, an expensive desk, wall-to-wall car-
peting, a television and wood panelling. Paradise on earth, when I
recalled the chilly old-fashioned studies the Church of England priests
endured back home in England. The minister received me graciously
wearing an expensive suit and red tie. Unknown to me, he had already
been threatened in the morning's mail that if he married John-Paul to
me, his church would be blown sky high.

Too sweetly he refused, adding insult to the injury. "If you want
each other so much, then just live together. Sometimes discretion is
best."

Discretion be damned. He didn't know my mother. That was not
what she had said. This clergyman, wearing an outrageous tie and no

clerical collar, had actually suggested we live in sin. Darkness was falling as I walked despondently back to Society Street. Then something miraculous and Old Testament-like happened. As I passed the convent an elderly black man stepped out from the shadows. "I am the Reverend William Singleton," he said. "I will marry you tomorrow."

I had never met the Rev. Singleton, ordained in the African Methodist Episcopal Church, although apparently we were neighbors. To me at that moment, he seemed sent by God. Mercifully for the soon-to-be-wed, the Rev. Singleton met with full approval from Mr. James, who insisted they were cousins. However, my outspoken old butler thought the bridal gown too low in the bodice when it arrived after a quick fitting at Rosalie Meyers' shop. The proprietor and a sales clerk, both well aware of the celebrities the event would make of them, were most helpful. Along with the gown of handmade white lace, which cost $1,000, there was a veil to be worn with one of my great-grandmother's Spanish mantillas. As with the best Charleston weddings, society florist Joe Trott did the flowers, sending to New York to get violets for my Victorian posy. John-Paul hated ties. So, Max's Men's Wear suggested a white turtle-neck shirt to wear with his new blue tuxedo. My wedding ring from Sears Roebuck was just like Lady Bird Johnson's. It cost $22.50.

Mr. James, of course, was in charge of arrangements. On the day of the wedding, he set out his gold watch chain, his two wedding rings (one from his wife and one from his girlfriend), his social fraternity ring with the great horned owl and his gold chastity bracelet (given to him by the girlfriend as a reminder should he think of getting frisky with some other filly) neatly on top of the Queen Anne dining room table. Anyone would have thought that he was the one getting married. Then he proceeded to polish everything, making me even more nervous than I already was, for the wedding was at 7 p.m. and there was still much to be done. Mr. James, however, was not about to be hurried; his adornments had to be polished along with his best church-going shoes. Meanwhile, I helped set out the cake and glasses in the mink coat Richia had given me as an engagement present, worn over my silk slip.

Finally, it was my turn for Mr. James's attentions. We set up Aunt Gertrude's small, ornate French ormolu table in the lower drawing room as a makeshift altar, placing Saint Teresa of Avila on the top. She had come a long way since leaving the cloistered convent of the Decalced Carmelite in Seville with Great-Grandmother, three generations before. There was a three-tiered wedding cake to set out and dozens of glasses, although only a few people had been officially invited. Mr. James's maxim was "Better safe than sorry." And, as it always turned out, he was right.

As for the bridegroom, he was noticeably absent, saying his fond farewells to Dorothy Nelson, his long-time girlfriend who lived in a nearby housing project. To her credit, she sent me a prenuptial message to remember that I was "the wife of the flesh." The term, popular among Charleston's black women, meant I had been chosen over other girlfriends.

I didn't realize what John-Paul's relationship with Dottie meant to the two of them. I was always blind where he was concerned.

It was January 21, 1969. All day long the local radio stations were alerting listeners that Charleston's wedding of the year (or any year) was about to take place. One of the television stations announced, "Have we got a story for you. Have we got a story!" The *New York Times* called to confirm that "Miss Hall was really getting married" wanting a note for the next day's society pages. *The Daily News*, whose leading columnist was my good friend Liz Smith, telephoned to ask if I was to wear the pearls that Dame Margaret had given me.

The street in front of the Old High School opposite was already filling with the curious. Larry Shelton, a leading Charleston hairdresser, arrived to do my hair accompanied by West Grant. Then, with the help of one of John-Paul's several sisters I started to dress in my antebellum bedroom upstairs. As Mother Rutherford would have said, "The stage is all set. Let the play begin."

We were nervous because John-Paul was late. The wedding was slated to begin at 7 p.m. A few minutes past, one of his brothers saw fit to announce, "If he doesn't show up, then I will have to marry you." I thanked him for his chivalrous offer, but I wasn't that desperate for a husband. Then, after what seemed like an eternity to me, waiting in my finery, a great cry went up from the crowd in the street; at last the bridegroom had come.

He seemed nervous but determined. I felt like Lorna Doone, who in the classic novel of that name was shot dead at the altar. I felt very much alone.

A prominent black lawyer, Bernard Fielding, also a friend of mine, had promised to give me away, but at the last moment developed political ambitions, leaving me standing alone at the top of the stairs. I wasn't alone long; up came John-Paul's father, who proudly gave me away.

To the stirring sounds of "The Battle Hymn of the Republic," Dawn Pepita Langley Hall, authoress, historian and preservationist, walked down like a lamb to the slaughter. There in the spacious lower drawing room amidst a sea of black faces I could see Mr. and Mrs. Maurice Krawchek, friends from Max's Men's Wear. Looking very solemn was Jack Leland, *The News and Courier* reporter.

At last, all the years of frustration and waiting were over. As I stood with John-Paul by Saint Teresa's little altar I felt relief.

Resplendent in white collar and red bib, the officiating clergyman looked more like a bishop. Then, as he told us to kneel, I remembered the hassocks; Mr. James had forgotten them. Well, all I can say is that when you have to kneel for a twenty-minute sermon on the marital virtues of Isaac and Rebecca on a hard pine wood floor, it is a test of endurance. To make matters worse, the mantilla was slipping. Would the Rev. Singleton never finish preaching and declare us man and wife?

Finally, it was over. Flashbulbs popped, the certificate was signed and television cameras whirred while a Japanese journalist loudly protested, about what I never found out. John-Paul led me upstairs. Mr. James threw open the doors to the piazza. And again the crowd roared; a woman shouted, "Throw it." Down went the bouquet with Joe Trott's precious violets. People were everywhere. Blinds that had remained closed all the years I had lived there, moved apart at the convent. Even the good nuns were caught up.

We traipsed downstairs again, this time to the dining room where Mr. James had arranged as a surprise his piéce de resistance. He had painted the plastic groom on our wedding cake black! Then suddenly, without warning, wearing Uncle Joseph Whitney's top hat, he threw open the front door to the crowd.

"Come in. Come in for Missus' champagne. Here, Ma'am, have some cake," he ordered, pushing a plate in a startled dowager's face.

"My missus got married! My missus got married!" Then, remembering the groom, Mr. James decided it was high time to assert himself.

"Big Shot," he shouted, "you may be her new husband, but I'm still the boss."

To make a long story short, the crowd drank all the champagne and ate most of the cake, but it was a good crowd. Afterwards, not one thing, in a house filled with valuable antiques, was found to be missing. They cheered us on our way as we left, horns blowing, for the dancing at Brooks Motel, a black-owned establishment. Shortly thereafter, the motel burned to the ground.

Overseas calls were made to my two mothers informing them of the wedding. At Sissinghurst Castle the phone was answered by Nigel Nicolson's children's nurse, Shirley Punnett who had disturbing news that Margie was in Hawkhurst Cottage Hospital, seriously ill with pneumonia. At Gerrard's Cross, those happy troubadours were enjoying their midnight breakfast of bacon and eggs just as in the old days when Mother returned late from a role at a West End theater. They were quite ecstatic at the news until Mother Rutherford asked, "Where were you married?" When I told her in my drawing room and the reason, she was furious.

"I am an English woman," she sniffed, in her best Miss Marple manner. "There is more than one way to skin a cat. I will call the Archbishop of Canterbury," which she did, getting his Grace out of bed at four in the morning. He was only too glad to promise her a second ceremony in a church.

At Brook's, where I belatedly learned that John-Paul couldn't dance (instead he did some kind of Elvis Presley shake), the reception was both pleasant and in good taste, but how glad I was when it was time to go home. As John-Paul admitted, "We are bone tired out." Upon arrival I got into my blue chiffon nightgown all ready for bed, but Mr. James refused to be hurried. First, he had to put out the garbage. Then Miss Jackie needed brushing. Then, he thought he deserved another drink. I suspected he had a bottle of champagne put aside for such an occasion. In desperation, John-Paul said, "Mr. James, sir, man to man, don't you understand this is my first night?"

Even this did not sway the indomitable major-domo who then, for some unknown reason, insisted we, me in my blue chiffon nightgown, take him home.

John-Paul agreed, just to get rid of him. But even that didn't work. Once there, the drink went to Mr. James's head and he fell to the ground, so John-Paul carried him bodily in. As we'd driven Mr. James' car, we then had to walk home. It's a wonder I wasn't arrested for indecent exposure.

Again, Mr. James had the last word. He had laid out a pair of expensive silk pajamas for the bridegroom and, whether from malice or forgetfulness, had left in all the pins. As John-Paul Simmons climbed General Robert E. Lee's bed steps he looked like a commercial for Band-Aids.

Aftermath

"Adam and Eve and Pinch Me
went down to the river to bathe.
Adam and Eve were drowned,
Now who do you think was saved?"
　　　　　　—Old Sussex Rhyme

Newsweek said I had shaken "the cradle of the Confederacy," but even it could not have been more shaken than I the day after the wedding, when my new father-in-law handed me a copy of his wife's medical history. It was headed, "Schizophrenia." I was in shock. I was not a jackass; I knew perfectly well what schizophrenia meant, that in some medical circles it was thought to be hereditary. I left John-Paul happily gluing a model airplane together in the dining room while I went and sat under the live oak with only the faithful Miss Jackie for company.

My thoughts were interrupted when Mr. James arrived with the newspapers. The New York *Daily News* had a photograph of John-Paul fixing the pearls at my neck. *The New York Times* was kind, placing me in the society pages like any other bride. Cousin Alexis sent over *The Savannah Morning News* with a very glamorous picture of me in full bridal regalia, headlined, "Mrs. John P. Simmons. Married." In Charleston, *The News and Courier* had a brief note on the obituary page. In Britain, because of Mother's popularity, we were front page news as in France, West Germany and, for some unknown reason, Japan. A Japanese magazine photographer took photographs of us, the newly-weds, at Charleston's Four Corners of Law. He gave us each a new camera and Mr. James a small radio. Nobody dared leave him out.

We had awakened that morning to find a motor car standing in front of the house adorned with white ribbons and a large card that read: "A Present From Richia." Although I couldn't drive and had never owned a car in my life, I was delighted. Next day, to my horror, our wedding gift was missing. John-Paul had given it to his brother. Morally, perhaps he had the right to do this; repugnant to me was what happened then, for his brother went straight to trade it in as a down payment on a flashy sports model.

Actually, I learned a very good lesson, for John-Paul could be over-ly generous with his own or his new wife's money. He had two rooms of new furniture picked out for his mother. The store owner phoned the house for me to come and pay for it. Even the black Baptist minister who had ducked out of marrying us saw fit to advise me, "With money, be prudent. Never tell your husband what you have in the bank."

When I bought John-Paul a newer Thunderbird model, Mr. James sagely said, "Missus, all we need is a sign reading 'TAXI.'" Truer words were never spoken, for John-Paul drove friends and relatives all over Charleston and beyond. When the gas tank was empty he came home for me to buy more.

Then he decided he wanted a fishing boat to earn money "to sup-port me," so I bought him a boat. He parked it with the others in Mosquito Creek where the old black men fished. Somebody must have been jealous, for three days later it was vandalized. Sand had been poured into the engine, by whom we never knew; some said by an old girlfriend. Years later, when Dena Crane was in Charleston filming our story, an old man pointed out the rusted shell of John-Paul's good intentions, sticking out of a mud bank, covered with reeds.

When it was found I needed minor surgery to enlarge the vaginal opening, I went to the hospital in Baltimore, where tidbits about us would not be leaked to the Charleston wire services. The doctors said it was a matter of three or four days, nothing to worry about. Five other newlywed women were there for exactly the same purpose as I. Of course, I had to be different, slipping on some ice the day I was admitted, and scratching a knee. Blood poisoning set in; I was there for a month. The big black nurse said it all when I was wheeled into surgery. "Honey, no man is worth it."

At least a letter from England cheered me.

Dear Dawn Pepita:

I am sorry for the infection in your leg and your being kept in the hospital longer than you expected. You are so brave, getting the publisher's work done in spite of everything! But you will soon be home now, and won't that be lovely?

My dear love to John-Paul. He is so far away, but you will soon be together again now, so take courage.

Ever,

Mother

Back at the mansion, John-Paul couldn't function without me. From a small house filled with competitive brothers and sisters, the transition was too much. To him, Mr. James proved worse than his own father, with moral indignation at all that he did. Each night when John-Paul telephoned the hospital it was worse than the last as he listed the disasters. Annabel-Eliza, the Chihuahua, had died, "grieving" for me. He had put her body in the refrigerator where Mr. James found it. He left a pot on the stove while he ran down to see Dottie, his lady friend in the projects, setting fire to the new kitchen. He sat on a Regency chair and the legs crumpled beneath him. Poor John-Paul, at least he was honest, he did tell me everything, but the doctors were furious for his upsetting their patient. In the end, he was forbidden to call.

John-Paul was John-Paul. There was nobody like him. He walked out of school at 12 and never went back. I taught him to read and write as years before in my childhood I taught Tony Stapley, a young neighbor. John-Paul gave me credit for providing his art books and taking him to museums and galleries, exposing him to a beauty he never knew could exist.

We were still good copy, even to our enemies who, unfortunately, controlled the local wire services. The informants were well paid for their half-truths.

John-Paul boasted while Mr. James gossiped. Unwittingly, they revealed what should have been kept secret. I had suddenly developed a passion for chocolate sauce.

Dear Margie, the pneumonia behind her, wrote on her flimsy blue airmail:

> I do hope your suspicions are wrong. It is far too soon.
> Don't let Aunty Doris Copper write and upset you. She
> doesn't like black people. "Too stuck up for someone who
> was only a maid." Some people are cruel. I keep telling
> them, "Dinky is ill."

Then the snoopy reporters got wind that Mr. James was knitting little things. (I never could knit, while he said it was easy as making fishnets on Edisto.) John-Paul and I were photographed in late February 1969, by one of the wire services, in the garden that Vita Sackville-West had designed, John-Paul holding up a little shirt, our old butler's creation. They loved it in London.

Richia Atkinson Barloga arrived from her home below Broad Street with the most magnificent maternity gowns, orange and purple, shocking pink and gold. She had found them all in a Columbia boutique. The trouble was they left little for the imagination, even with a silk slip underneath.

"Waiting for the ship to come in," was the caption of a fattened-up Dawn standing with John-Paul's lunch on the shaky old dock at Mosquito Creek. I never did find him. (I should have called Miss Dottie's.) But, the press photographers got an eyeful of me.

News from the two mother fronts gradually worsened. For some unknown reason, the British tax people decided that as I owned Beecholme, Margie's lost childhood home, bought back into the family with my royalties, I was liable for taxes over there as well as in America.

This I could not afford. If Margie had moved in fulltime, leaving the hated Sissinghurst behind her, then the tax man would not have classed it as my main residence, which it wasn't. But Margie, even at that point in their lives, couldn't leave Jack, even for part of the week, even though he could have spent weekends with her. Beecholme was a scant 20 miles away.

The tax man was adamant, forcing me to sell Beecholme for a fraction of its worth. Margie never got over the second loss of Beecholme.

Beloved actresses cannot always hold onto their money, even though, as in Mother Rutherford's case after the first Miss Marple movie, she had become the highest paid star at MGM. For years the income tax people had been ready to pounce on her. It was well known that at one time she had threatened to lead a march on the Houses of Parliament to protest the high taxes. Only a personal call from Winston Churchill had stopped her.

She bought Elm Close, paying the full price in cash. She was generous to an extreme to anyone with a hard luck story. She was the eternal optimist. She always thought she could work. She had won her Oscar as a senior citizen of 72! But time was running out.

She was filming in Italy when her productivity came to a grinding halt. Father Stringer called *Arabella* "the film in which Margaret got to wear all of those beautiful clothes." As an aging princess, she was ably supported by the Italian actress Virna Lisi, whose most beautiful manners impressed her, and Terry Thomas, that most British of comedians.

Mother always insisted a cameo role be found for Father in all of her films; even Orson Welles had had to comply in his production, *Chimes at Midnight*, filmed in Spain. There was no one more British in ways or appearance than Father Stringer, but in Rome he found himself cast as an Italian gardener, neckerchief knotted like a tie at his throat.

Life in Italy was difficult for both of them after their quiet regime at Elm Close, although the Villa Floria set in the Frascati Hills where they stayed was particularly beautiful. Nobody seemed to speak English, and they couldn't understand Italian. "There was the question of our early morning tea," Mother Rutherford complained, "without which I cannot move my legs."

"We never did get our tea at the hour we most needed it and sometimes they sent it in a teapot big enough for a family of eight." As for their beloved bacon and eggs, that situation was even worse. "We got eggs and ham in every form, but seldom plain, as we were used to having."

Consequently, they both felt rather ungracious when the Consorzio Stampa Cinematografica presented Mother with a medal called "A Life for the Cinema" at the Brigadoon nightclub in Rome.

They went home to Elm Close for a few weeks rest and proper bacon, before returning to Rome for the dubbing. Two days later, Mother fell in her hotel bedroom and broke her hip. At the Salvator Mundi Hospital, the doctors begged her to stay quietly with her injured hip in plaster for a month.

"If only we had listened," Father Stringer was often to lament.

"I was determined to come home," Mother Rutherford explained. She was flown back to London, being carried on and off the plane by stretcher, as the *Daily Mail* reported, "So that the operation could be performed in this country." When advised to sue the hotel in Rome, her reply was very Margaret Rutherfordish, "That would be most ungracious."

John-Paul and I were now sleeping in a small bedroom over what had been the old kitchen. John-Paul felt more at home in informal surroundings. The small house on Montague Court where he'd spent most of his childhood was about the same size as this former carriage house was. It was a cool morning July 23, 1969, and nearly time to get up. I was not ready for the bombshell.

"I have something to tell you," John-Paul said as he sat up and looked down at me. "My son was born last night at the hospital."

"Your son?" I froze. "Dottie," I mumbled. Nobody had even told me she was expecting.

He nodded, then took hold of my hand, but I wrenched it away. He looked hurt.

"No need to upset yourself. You paid for it," and with that final remark he got out of bed. I was frozen with the sense of betrayal.

By the time he came back, bringing me some coffee, I was calm. My thoughts were of the new baby, so tiny and innocent. As Margie would have said in her gentleness, "He didn't ask to be born." Then I remembered that other child at the bungalow, Havana. Could I ever forget the day the priest couldn't find my baptismal record and I learned that I had been illegitimate? Well, this child was not going through that; not my stepson.

"John-Paul," I said, and he knew I meant it, "I shall never understand why you married me when that woman was in trouble. Now go down to the court house and give him our name."

I might have been a late bloomer, but I was growing up fast.

There had been two letters from Sissinghurst that week, Margie's more cheerful than usual. She had decided on pink to wear to our second marriage ceremony in Hastings. "But please don't make me wear a corsage. I look like a dwarf in a corsage." Sissinghurst was no longer her prison, thanks to Philippa Nicolson, Nigel Nicolson's wife, who let her work at the castle gate, admitting visitors. Now part of the National Trust, its beautiful gardens were opened daily to the public. Mrs. Nicolson told her she could sell more postcards to the Americans than anyone. Like my other mother, Margie had a great affinity for the New World. She also helped out by caring for Mrs. Nicolson's sick dog, Rip. She was often too busy to really do so, sometimes with dire consequences. Once, Greta Garbo was coming to the castle for lunch, and Margie was determined to catch a glimpse of the screen legend. In her excitement, Margie took two of Rip's seizure pills thinking they were aspirins. She was quite insulted when Jack suggested they send for the vet!

The Nicolson children, Juliet and Adam, often dropped by with their projects, for Margie always had time for them. "We all made an airplane out of cardboard," she wrote me, "with me supplying the glue."

Sadly, the other letter was a stranger ordering me to leave Margie in peace, that she had suffered enough. I had never met the woman. Margie had never mentioned her. Later I was told she was connected with an antique shop at Goudhurst. Whoever she was—and God knows—she had access to my address. I decided not to tell Margie. I just wouldn't write for a week. By then, it would be too late.

A group of Mother Rutherford's fans wanted to visit, so one day late in August we arranged a small tour of the two drawing rooms, dining room and our little garden. They were such a jolly group, so appreciative of our efforts to welcome them. Even Mr. James liked them as he posed for his picture by a magnolia tree. I remember that day, etched dagger-like in my memory, even the dress of yellow organdy I was wearing. We had reached the upper drawing room when one of the New England group recognized the pine highboy from Connecticut, so different from the mahogany ones popular in old Charleston homes. I showed him the maker's initial under a drawer. He explained the historical merits of the piece to the group, which pleased me to no end for nobody had ever really appreciated it but me. Then Mr. James came in with Cousin Isabel's silver salver on which lay a letter from England which, half-listening to my guest, I absent-mindedly opened. Inside was a sympathy card from my cousin Gwen Macnamara of Heathfield. My poor sweet Margie was dead.

I remember no more; for when I woke up, I was in a hospital bed.

As I lay immersed in my own world of confusion the doctors feared for my mind. When I asked if the baby was all right they only nodded, and so, satisfied, I would sink back into a void. Then one night when the hospital was quiet, my mind suddenly cleared and I brutally remembered that Margie was dead.

Then from England the sad details came.

She had worked all morning admitting visitors to the garden, then at noon had gone into her own house to prepare Jack some lunch. She left his plate, ready to eat, on the kitchen table, then, going into the bedroom, closed the door and lay down on her bed. Jack, hearty and hungry, came in and ate, oblivious to the fact that his wife had suffered a cerebral hemorrhage behind that unpainted oak door. When at last she was found, they took her to Pembury Hospital where she passed away quite peacefully.

If Cousin Gwen hadn't sent me that card I would not have known Margie was dead. Had I known, I certainly would have flown to the funeral. After all, she was my natural mother and, as Barbara Van Kampen, the Dutch illustrator/author, wrote me, "What a tragedy to have a daughter she had never seen."

Mrs. Nicolson, later Lady McAlpine, in a letter to Jack, dwelt on Margie's "kindness to dogs and little children" in that order. Margie was buried at Sissinghurst under a gray granite Cornish cross.

"She Hath Done What She Could" was the text I chose for it.

Margie's death was compounded by the truth about my baby, born three months premature, dead. Because of the fragile state of my mind, I had been led to believe the child had been born and was all right. Later, I recalled hearing a black nurse exclaim, "This is a white man's child." A sister-in-law, more enterprising than the others, sold the news for $10 to a local radio station where it was picked up by a large London newspaper. It was awful for Mother Rutherford, convalescing at Elm Close. For two glorious days she blissfully thought she was a grand-mother.

Of course, in essence she was. The ashes of Bathsheba Marjorie Simmons lie in their tiny urn in my campaign desk in Hudson covered with a tiny silk flag of the Confederacy that Cousin Alexis sent me. Whoever goes first, John-Paul or I, the urn will go with that one to rest beside Margie.

Marjorie Hall Copper (Margie), Dawn's biological mother, at age 40.

Gordon Langley Hall, 18 months old, with Spot. (Photo credit: Gwendoline Martha Burgess)

THE

ENCHANTED

BUNGALOW

BY

GORDON LANGLEY HALL

Drawing by Cousin Helena Hall, aged 87. Gordon, aged 10, waves goodbye to Nelly with Havana in background.

Gordon as a teenager, with bull terrier, Regina.

Dr. Geoffrey Francis Fisher, Archbishop of Canterbury, at Lambeth Palace after discussion of *Saraband for a Saint.* (1957-8) (Photo credit: Dawn Langley Simmons)

Isabel Lydia Whitney, painter.

Isabel Lydia Whitney.

Gordon Langley Hall in
New York City.

Gordon Langley Hall
with Bette Davis in
Camden, Maine. (1957)
(Photo credit:
Emeline K. Paige and
Janet Hutchinson)

Portrait of Gordon by Lady Wilkins, wife of Arctic explorer Sir Hubert Wilkins.

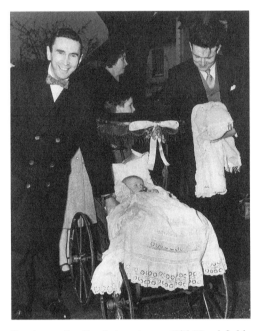

Gordon at family christening at Old Heathfield Church. (Photo credit: Roger Pain)

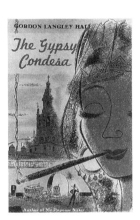

Gordon in New York. Bookjacket photo from *The Gypsy Condesa*. (Macrae Smith Publishers)

Gordon at the
Whitney House.
Bookjacket photo
from *Princess
Margaret, An Informal
Biography*. (Macrae
Smith Publishers)

Gordon and Margaret
Rutherford at dedication of
Anglo-American friendship win-
dow, Old Heathfield Church.
(Photo credit: Roger Pain)

Gordon and Mother Rutherford planting a poplar tree at Beecholme. (Photo credit: Roger Pain)

Gordon and pets, 1969. (Photo credit: Margaret Rummel)

The Dr. Joseph Johnson House, 56 Society Street in Charleston under renovation.

Dining Room of 56 Society Street, 1969. (Photo credit: Margaret Rummel)

"Mr. James" Fickling with cousin Rosabelle Ten Cents Waite, daughter of Natasha's nurse, Evelyn Bernell.

Dawn Langley Hall, 1968.

Dawn Langley Hall, 1969.
(From the collection of Alexis Kalinowsky)

Dawn Langley Simmons with
Miss Jackie, her German
Shepherd, in front of 56 Society
Street, Charleston.
(Photo credit: Julian Metz)

Dawn Langley
Simmons and John-
Paul Simmons at City
Hall in Charleston,
1969.

Dawn Langley Simmons wedding portrait. (Photo credit: Chateau Gabriel)

John-Paul and Dawn at their wedding in Hastings, England. (Photo credit: Sydney Morning News, Australia)

John-Paul and Dawn with Mother Rutherford at their Hastings wedding, Nov. 7, 1969.

Cousin Nigel Burgess with bride, Maureen. Nigel was best man at the Hastings wedding and the couple later became Natasha's godparents. Nigel was also Damian's godfather.

Dawn pregnant with
Natasha in 1971.

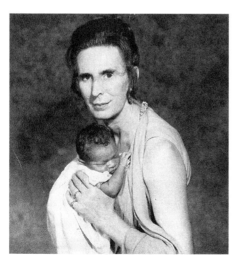

Copy of Natasha
Marginell
Manigault Paul
Simmons's birth
certificate.

Dawn with Natasha.

Natasha's christening at St. Clement's Hastings with godparents Philip Savins, Patricia Ivings, Walter Henshaw, Dawn with Natasha, Stringer Davis, Mrs. Vere Littleton, and Maureen Burgess.

Dawn at the Rutherford grave, St. James Churchyard, Gerrards Cross, England.

Dawn with Natasha.
(Photo credit: Chateau Gabriel)

Dawn and Natasha at St. Clement's
Rectory, Hastings. 1979. (Photo credit:
Philip Savins)

Lemuel Smith.

Natasha Marginell Manigault
Simmons

Dawn and John-Paul in
Albany, N.Y. 1982.

Dawn Sad by John-Paul Simmons.
(Martin Birnbaum collection)

John-Paul with Damian
in 1988.

Damian Patrick Hall Simmons, aged 2, 1989.

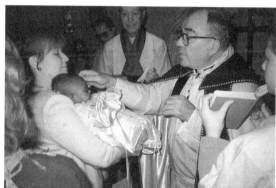

The Bishop of Albany, The Right Rev. David S. Ball baptizes Tamara Miquel Hall Simmons at Christ Church, Hudson, N.Y. Dec. 8, 1991. Godmother Helene Gardner holds baby.

Dawn and family, Thanksgiving Day 1992, at Tivoli, N.Y. home of Paul Bergtold and Kent Brown, formerly of Charleston. (Photo credit: Kelly Bugden)

The Most Beautiful Day
Of My Life

*"Those whom God hath joined
together let no man put asunder."*
From the Church of England's
Solemnization of Matrimony

Mother Rutherford waited until late fall for the Church of
England's approval of my marriage to John-Paul. Finally, she
could send out printed invitations for a second marriage ceremony to be
held on November 9, 1969, after which there would be a grand reception at the Alexandra Hotel in nearby St. Leonard's-on-Sea. Hastings
was chosen. Tom Savins, formerly vicar of Old Heathfield, was now rector there, officiating in the historic 12th century St. Clement's Parish
Church. Set in the old part of the town with its fine period houses that
led down to the fishing boats and sea, it was a dream setting for anybody's wedding. Now all we had to do was get our bodies there in one
piece from belligerent Charleston. There was still hardly a day that we
didn't get anonymous threats by telephone or mail.

The night before we were due to fly to England there was a terrible
rainstorm in the Holy City, so bad that one of John-Paul's former lady
friends fell headfirst and drowned in a puddle of water. Of course, wedding or not, he had to be the first, in his Thunderbird, to offer condolences.

"Where is Miss Dawn?" I shall never know why I was so necessary on such emotional occasions. John-Paul explained that as he was the only black man to have a white wife, it was sort of prestigious for him to have me along. So I paid my condolences and returned alone to my packing, John-Paul insisting he still had to make some final goodbyes. Unfortunately, it was still pouring and he was wearing a brand new brown suit with which Max's Men's Wear had so helpfully supplied him. They always dressed him beautifully. When at last he returned, he was soaked to the skin, but there was no time to change for we had to rush straight to the airport. By the time we reached London his new outfit had shrunk.

We were met at Heathrow by author Gwen Robyns, kindly acting as liaison officer for the wedding. Seeing John-Paul in a wrinkled suit that seemed several sizes too small, Gwen quickly decided that it was not the best time to meet waiting photographers. Instead, we were whisked out a back door, then driven straight to the Waldorf Hotel where my adoptive parents were waiting.

For John-Paul, who had never been out of his native Charleston except for a brief visit to Washington when I had opened an art show, it was one great new adventure. Mother Rutherford and Father Stringer were waiting for us in a private suite. They were overjoyed to see us. He was very dapper but still smoking too much. Ill-health had taken its toll on Mother Rutherford, who had visibly lost weight and grown smaller. She appeared to be older than the last time I'd seen her. John-Paul's kind heart and respect for older people really manifested itself with Mother. They liked each other from the start. In several photographs he is shown holding her hand. Later he made a folk-sculpture of her, using concrete as a medium. Sadly, he felt bound to depict his mother-in-law as he remembered her, with bent legs, leaning on two sticks for support.

In spite of her infirmity, she had just been voted the best foreign actress in Germany, so one of that country's leading picture magazines, *Neue Revue*, gave us a beautiful prenuptial luncheon with a table centerpiece of pink Cornish anemones and large purple asters. Even then I thought of purple Aunt Gertrude.

I don't think John-Paul ever forgot the German literary agent who, thinking we might need money in London, paid me in cash for the German picture rights to the Hastings ceremony sold by Mother Rutherford to *Neue Revue*. I have never seen so many £10 notes in my life. Somewhat embarrassed, I stuffed them into my purse.

I liked Gwen Robyns from the moment we met, a marvelous choice to arrange our second wedding. She had helped Mother Rutherford write her autobiography under the most difficult of circumstances, Father stopping her from using vital material about William Rutherford, Mother's ill-fated father. This was hard enough on a factual writer, but then Gwen would be fast asleep in bed at Elm Close when Father would knock on her door, calling out, "Bacon-and-egg time," in the most cheerful of voices. Gwen would later write an excellent biography of Princess Grace of Monaco.

Next day Mother was in good mettle, with a few bones to pick. She had been incensed by some of the cheap sex stories that had been issued from Charleston to some of the more flamboyant British tabloids. So she took me to visit Dr. Elliot Phipps, the eminent British gynecologist, who declared in a written statement published on the front page of *The People*, "In my opinion she has always been a woman and can have more children. It is a tragedy that she was wrongly sexed at birth."

Then there was tea with the Archbishop of Canterbury, on which occasion John-Paul, drawing on his natural Carolina Lowcountry grass roots philosophy, intrigued and delighted His Grace. "Of me," John-Paul said in his simple, proud way, "I know the kind of woman she is. I can trust her." How I wished our detractors had been present at Lambeth Palace, the official residence of the Archbishop of Canterbury, that pleasant afternoon.

On Sunday, in bright sunshine after a night of heavy rain, I drove with John-Paul through the streets of London on the way to Cousin Rosy's home, Cauldomer, Marle Green, Horam, in my own native Sussex, where I was to dress ready for Hastings. On billboards everywhere, even tied to lamp posts, was my photograph with large words that declared to the world, "She Can Have Children!"

How I loved my Mother Rutherford that day. "She can have children." What a beautiful wedding gift.

When I was little I always told Cousin Rosy that if I ever got married she would attend me, even though she was of Margie's generation and not mine. The day of my second wedding, she darted around like a little firecracker in her long sea-green gown. As always, she was the life of the party. Mother and Father liked her immediately, as she whisked out a model fire engine to give them. "I have always wanted to ride to a fire on the engine," Mother said. "Perhaps, my dear, you will take me—when my legs have recovered, of course." Mother Rutherford, who was a child at heart, had found in our Rosy a kindred spirit.

John-Paul was intrigued by a pair of tall porcelain vases in the drawing room at Cauldomer with life-size birds sticking out of the sides. He had developed good taste. They were Meissen.

Then my cousin Nigel Burgess arrived in his bright red sports car to be John-Paul's best man. Together they sped off to Hastings. John-Paul looked so handsome in his neat black tuxedo with real lace cravat (Father Stringer convinced him to wear it) and cuffs.

Upstairs, the hairdresser from the Waldorf, who had traveled down from London, dressed my hair and fastened the veil in place with Mother Rutherford's diamond tiara, the same one that she'd worn as the Grand Duchess Gloriana XIII in *Mouse on the Moon*, her astronaut movie.

Then it was my turn. As Father Stringer's full attention was needed on assisting Mother on sticks, my cousin Patricia's husband, handsome bearded Derek Ivings, gave me away. As we drove in a real London taxi through grassy lanes where I'd cycled and picked wild primroses in childhood, I thought of my grandmother and of Margie and, of course, dear Aunty Doom. The Hall family motto was fulfilled like a prophesy:

"Nothing Is Impossible With The Lord."

I knew then that it wasn't.

St. Clement's Parish Church nestled at the foot of green cliffs with castle ruins overhead; it was a storybook setting. Unfortunately, the London taxi driver got hopelessly lost and we finished up on a road high above the town while down below the bells of St. Clement's rang furiously. It was very frustrating. I was 40 minutes late. I felt so sorry for John-Paul and Nigel standing up all that time.

Our old friend, the Rev. Tom Savins, was waiting at the great west door with the greeting, "We only open it for VIPs." I quickly put on Margie's green jade earrings, which my sister Fay had sent Tom to give me. Then, turning in the theatrical gown of golden brocade with leg of mutton sleeves together with a long gold velvet train designed for me by David Stokes II, I faced a fully robed choir and the processional cross, carried by Tom's youngest son, Philip, in a crimson cassock. "Lead us, heavenly Father, lead us o'er the world's tempestuous sea..." We were passing now up the long aisle of the cathedral-like church and there, with Cousin Nigel, my dear John-Paul was waiting. Both were smiling their heads off.

"Dearly beloved, we are gathered together in the sight of God and in the face of this congregation to join together this man and this woman in Holy Matrimony..." Mother always did say that Tom Savins had missed his true calling; with that splendid diction he should have been an actor. Then, suddenly, came a familiar voice from behind, and everyone—priest, bride, groom and congregation—paused to listen. It was Mother Rutherford who turned to her audience as if she were on stage. "Oh, isn't it wonderful! Isn't it wonderful!" she cried, rubbing both hands together while Father supported her. The congregation-turned-audience were caught up in the act, and, forgetting where they were, began to applaud.

Resplendent in her gown of silvery blue with the hat of blue osprey feathers, which she'd worn to Buckingham Palace when the Queen had made her a Dame, Mother, in her element, was on stage again. Then, after so unique an interruption, our wedding continued. The only catastrophe was a loud crash when Roger Pain, an old photographer friend, dropped his camera on the flagstones, smashing it to smithereens. Tom had skillfully hidden 22 photographers, employed by news organizations around the world, behind the choir screen. The full choir and bell ringers likewise had volunteered their services as a gesture of good will to John-Paul and me. It was all very touching.

Slowly we walked up to the altar, me carefully manipulating the long train that by rights needed several pages to carry it. We knelt while the choir sang that most lovely of bridal hymns, "O Perfect Love." A year later, at lunch in the rectory, Tom would tell me that as we knelt he looked down to admire the bridegroom's elegant tuxedo, then noticed his cowboy boots! Said the Rector of Hastings, "All I could think of was Nancy Sinatra singing 'Those Boots Were Made For Walking.' The thought simply came over me."

Finally, the strains of "The Wedding March" concluded the service as the church bells rang out triumphantly. As we passed through the west door the wind caught up my veil, to the delight of the cameras. There were relatives and friends of a lifetime, but none more welcome than the last of my grandmother's living friends, Elsie Carter, cousin of Kitty Scott, the Spicers' once bald-headed maid.

The festivities continued at the Alexandra Hotel, from whose windows the English Channel could be seen. Margaret Savins, Tom's always helpful wife, had collaborated in choosing the wedding cake with Mother Rutherford, who'd insisted on hard icing on the top. It was surely the happiest day of my life. Sadly, good things come to an end. We had to return to our home in Charleston.

On the following day it was Father Stringer's turn, as he created the bridal luncheon in his kitchen at Elm Close. *His* because nobody else was allowed in that sacred domain. Even fellow actor Robert Morley told me that when he and Mother were visiting in the drawing room they had to talk in whispers so as not to "disturb Stringer while he was buttering his scones."

The dining room was set up with the best Rockingham china for the feast of roast beef and potatoes, the traditional English meal Father wanted John-Paul to remember. Then, afterwards, he took his new son-in-law for a walk in the garden, while Mother chortled happily in her best Rutherfordish manner, "Oh, I do hope they like each other." They did, and when John-Paul returned he was holding a single red rose, which he gave me with a kiss.

"I've been teaching him how to be a background husband," Father

Stringer said, knowing only too well what that meant. What Father never understood, Molly Parkin, the British journalist did. Of John-Paul and me she knowingly wrote, "He is an extrovert while she is an introvert."

Reprisals

W hen we reached home the reprisals were frightening. Even now, more than 20 years later, they return in my worst nightmares to haunt me. Always there is fire, and for good reason.

Our wedding presents arrived from England in two large crates. As it was late afternoon, we decided to leave them inside the driveway ready to unpack the next day. We never had the chance, for that night somebody threw a firebomb over the iron gates, setting them on fire. Sleeping in the back bedroom of the carriage house we heard nothing until Miss Jackie began to bark frantically, waking us both. The smoke was overpowering. John-Paul ran to the windows, opened them, then cried out, "The driveway's on fire. We're being burned in our beds."

Somehow we managed to get out in our nightclothes with Miss Jackie following behind. Not only could we have been murdered in our beds but so could our elderly neighbor, Catherine Theresa Salmonsen, for old Charleston homes are built very close together.

Who called the fire house around the corner on Meeting, I never did know, but firefighters arrived in record time to put out the blaze in the trees and vines and crates in the driveway. Our house and Mrs.

Salmonsen's were both saved. The firemen raked the burned crates with their pathetic charred contents outside the gates, piling them into a heap. Lost were fine linens, two Hepplewhite side chairs and several oil paintings. I was numb. Next morning, to add insult to injury, the police chief himself turned up on his motorcycle to give me a ticket for obstructing the sidewalk.

The reprisals continued. Richia Atkinson Barloga gave John-Paul a Belgian shepherd named Peter, of whom he was very proud. One evening after dark, returning home to the mansion, shots rang out. The gunfire missed John-Paul, but killed his dog. I shall never forget the grief on his face as he carried that poor dead animal in. "Never mind," he said. "God knows who did it and God will repay."

It seemed fate that a day or two later Pierre Berton, the Canadian writer and television commentator, invited us to Toronto to film two interviews with him, all expenses paid. After the fire and Peter's murder—for, brought up to love animals as I had been, to me it was murder—I think that Pierre, who had known me for years because of my three books on Canadian Indians, saved my reason. As part of the agreement, John-Paul and I were allowed to stay overnight in Montreal on our way home to visit briefly with my cousins, Midge Ticehurst and her second husband David Chisolm. We did two filmed interviews with Pierre Berton in Toronto, one with me alone, the other together. It would be many years before I would see them when they were shown as part of an exhibition of John-Paul's folk sculptures in Woodstock, New York. It was nice for our daughter, Natasha Manigault Simmons, who had never known her father when his mind was well, to see him young and handsome as he was when I first knew him.

"Why did you marry her?" Mr. Berton asked.

"I wanted her dogs," John-Paul replied.

Back again to Charleston we went because John-Paul insisted. "I was born there and I'm not going to leave." In earnest, Father Stringer and Mother Rutherford begged us to come home to England. Things were deteriorating at Elm Close with little domestic help and money growing scarce. She had always been the main earner but was now too sick to act. He was devoting himself to nursing her. Financially, I did what I could, but still Father Stringer wrote to complain, "We are very lonely. Where are all the people?" The cruel fact was that even old friends could not bear to see their beloved Margaret Rutherford crippled.

Anonymous letters were arriving at 56 Society Street in 1969 and 1970, warning us to move, while a large, valuable historic plaque, made by Burslem Monumental Makers of Turnbridge Wells, England, disappeared (with the help of a chisel) from the front of the house.

Ansonborough, once derelict and neglected, was becoming one of the most fashionable of Charleston's historic neighborhoods. Poor black and white families had gradually moved out, to be replaced by moneyed people who could afford to restore those same old buildings. These newcomers called it "gentrification." I do not recall a single black family being sold a house in Ansonborough during my residence. In 1989, the house next door to my former residence was priced for sale at $350,000 with major repairs still to be done.

With John-Paul as a husband and the prospect of half-black offspring, I was now classed as black. Some reactions were actually funny.

On a plane to New York I was given the seat next to an old white lady who promptly asked me my name.

"Mrs. Simmons," I replied.

"Which one of the Simmons boys did you marry, my dear?"

"The black one," I truthfully replied.

She spent the next 20 minutes in the bathroom.

Sadly, however, the conspiracy to remove the Simmonses had begun.

Where Did Honor Go?

> *"The lodestar of their lives was
> 'the point of honor.' A man's word
> must be better than his bond,
> because unguaranteed. A woman's
> name must never pass his lips
> except in respect; a promise, how*
> *ever foolish, must be kept."*
>
> Mrs. St. Julien Ravenel
> in *Charleston: The Place and the People*

I was having second thoughts. It wasn't just my marriage; it was the injustice of others. It was everything.

Nobody put it better than Mrs. St. Julien Ravenel. It was this code of honor that attracted me to Charleston. It was the same code of honor under which my own family, the Halls, had lived for centuries in Withyham, England, to say nothing of Mother Rutherford and Father Stringer. It might sound old-fashioned, but to us it was inviolate. This was the real reason that I married John-Paul. I obeyed the Church of England and my mothers. There was simply no way they could approve of us living in sin.

Would that the people responsible for our downfall, the destruction of my poor husband's mind, had considered these time-proven principles and judged us according to what was in our hearts rather than the color of our skins.

They would not. They wanted us off of Society Street. They wanted my house. What they didn't know was that 56 Society Street and all of the contents had been left to the Historic Charleston Foundation in a will drawn up by my attorney, Henry S. Edmunds, the husband of the foundation's director, Frances R. Edmunds. With my family's lifelong interest in saving historic homes, I was, and still am, totally committed to such worthy endeavors. Ashley Cooper, writing in his widely read *News and Courier* column, called me a preservationist a few years ago. I was pleased with his pronouncement.

My house was such an historic dwelling, a part of Charleston's inviolate heritage. It belonged to future generations and we, as a family, were the present custodians. As Read Barnes, our architect, told me, "Every generation should leave something of itself in a house." I put in French windows opening out into the gardens as my contribution.

I knew that John-Paul would never willingly leave his native city. Any native Charlestonian understands that. I, too, had fallen prey to the city's charm. In spite of all that happened later, I still am, as is our daughter, deeply attached to Charleston. Sadly though, I had come to the unhappy conclusion that it would be best to leave Ansonborough. Besides, there were other fine homes to be saved in other parts of the city. All I asked was a little time and a fair market price. Both considerations were denied me.

What in fact happened reads now like a mystery. How, looking back, could it ever have happened? Now, with a popular black police chief in Charleston, the finest of mayors, and a city highly protective of its tourist trade, I don't think it would. But I had married John-Paul in 1969, the tail end of the volatile Civil Rights Era.

There was a mortgage. I had borrowed money to refurbish the carriage house as a gallery for the pleasure of local residents and visitors, with its permanent collection of Cousin Isabel's watercolors. This gesture of neighborliness would come back like a slap in the face.

I'd gotten behind on payments. The loan institution suddenly called in the $18,000 mortgage balance. With helping my parents, sending money to my natural father who was now a semi-invalid, a young husband who did not understand the value of money, there was little ready cash flow. The amount needed to satisfy the mortgage was not large by present standards, but 20 years ago it seemed to be.

What I should have done was to have taken one work of art out of the mansion and sold it, but I had willed everything to Historic Charleston Foundation and thought I had no right. I then knew the meaning of my grandmother's favorite saying, "Between the devil and the deep blue sea."

It is not my nature to lose a battle quietly, so I fought back. Another creditor crawled out of the woodwork. He was a contractor who had reaped thousands of dollars to restore my house, plus the publicity, for it had been written up in several nationally read publications in the mid 1960s. He sent in a large bill for work on the carriage house roof which was so unsatisfactory it sagged in the middle like a fish pond. I actually took photographs of little duckling-like creatures swimming on my gallery top to produce when I went into court. My attorney then was Brantley Seymour, who had offices on Broad Street. To me he was God-sent like that other Southern lawyer with a conscience in the popular novel, *To Kill a Mocking Bird*. Mr. Brantley knew truth when he heard it. The contractor lied himself silly as did his foreman, who, confronted, couldn't look me in the face without blushing scarlet. Of course, it was all about money. The contractor would have lost future lucrative contracts, and by telling the truth, the foreman his job. We lost, but "with our honor intact," Mr. Brantley said. We had our day in court, but like a rotting alligator found in scenic Colonial Lake, it stank!

In order to move out of Ansonborough I had to have money to buy us a home in another part of the city, and, as anybody selling property knows, this is not done quickly. There were some friends left; although sometimes their good intentions added fuel to the flames. Such was Richia Atkinson Barloga who had given us the ill-fated car for a wedding present. A small, fiery, red-haired lady with an impeccable Louisiana background, she suddenly announced to her startled "below Broad Street" neighbors that she was giving me her Gibbes Street house as a gift. While telephones rang and the plot thickened, John-Paul and

I were oblivious to the news. When we did find out, I declined. My husband then asked, "Besides, I've never fished below Broad. Couldn't we just move out to Edisto?"

So the Society Street house was put on the market with certain realtors scenting "a distress sale." It wasn't, really; all that was needed to move with dignity was time. Considering the thousands of pioneer dollars I had sunk into Ansonborough, surely this courtesy wasn't too much to ask. I felt betrayed.

If I hadn't been worried half to death some things would have been funny. One of the city's leading woman realtors (John-Paul told me then that she wasn't a lady), arrived with her male client and a shoe box full of small bits of cotton. While I showed the client over the house, she went, uninvited, to my garden where she proceeded to tie cotton rags to the "camellias I am claiming as part of my commission." The only satisfaction I ever got from this sordid little saga was the knowledge that her client didn't get the house, or she my camellias!

The most promising buyer was a building contractor from Virginia, who was impressed with the good copper piping Read Barnes had installed throughout the house. He returned to Virginia to bring back his wife, but somehow word got around that I had a buyer, and a builder at that. Before he had time to return with his spouse my heart had been broken. 56 Society was sold on the steps of the court house, just as the Simmons, Snype and Vanderhorst slave-ancestors of my black husband had been. It was bargain day at the court house when a Charleston lawyer and his wife were the ecstatic new owners. The house sold for $45,000, $13,000 of which went to satisfy the mortgage. The rest was divided between my creditors and me.

The new owners began moving in. I came back from seeking other accommodations only to find art and antiques, including the George Washington mirrors, piled up like junk on the lower piazza. "Good God," Richia said. "We must be living in the Bronx; this *cannot* be Charleston!"

Sadly it was, while antique dealers crawled like carpetbaggers to see what they could inveigle at bargain prices. The money from the sale of the house was not enough to support us after the down payment for the Thomas Street house. I realized that the contents of 56 Society Street still belonged to me, and felt I owed The Historic Charleston Foundation nothing since it hadn't helped save anything. So, to raise immediate cash, I parted with some small works of art, never forgetting the good dealer who wouldn't finalize the deal unless his wife got the Staffordshire cat that had stood beside Saint Teresa's statue for four generations.

"To sweeten the pot," he said with a grin.

Justice Delayed Is
Still Justice Denied

"I tell this tale which is strictly true. Just by way of convincing you."

Rudyard Kipling

John-Paul, frightened by events, hurried home to his mother. Mother Rutherford was dying thousands of miles away. I spent one last night at "the pink palace" (as Gussie familiarly called it) with antiques and paintings piled like so much garbage on the porch. The next morning, I walked away carrying Saint Teresa. Miss Jackie followed me. To the end she never deserted me. As Margie once said, "Dogs show more loyalty than some people." We checked into a Calhoun Street motel, as I had no other place to go before moving into 17 Thomas Street, a neglected house, with at least 20 broken window panes, in a poor neighborhood.

John-Paul turned up a few days later, as he would always turn up, followed by furniture. Miraculously, the Washington mirrors were intact. We slept for three days. The events of the past few days had been so traumatic we were utterly exhausted. As Mr. James said, when he finally arrived on his rickety bicycle, "plumb worn out." Although I was no longer able to afford him, he kept in touch with me until his death in 1989. He spoke of his "Missus" to the last.

In a city where historic homes are treated like members of the family, losing one into which you have poured heart and soul was wrench-ing. Houses were always important to the Hall family, who had lived in their half-timbered house Duckings, Withyham, for many generations. They were there in 1601 and probably for many years before. When, in 1911, that long tenure came to an end, Richard Jeffries, the writer, likened that awful separation to "tearing up a mandrake by the roots."

I thought of those words when I lost the Dr. Joseph Johnson House forever.

It was April 1971, and in spite of our recent troubles, we were over-joyed; for God's sweetest gift, a child, was coming!

I might well have lost her like Bathsheba due to a craving for pigs' feet which John-Paul bought in a mostly black section of the city.

We had upset more people by agreeing to appear on stage with Mrs. Martin Luther King when she came to Charleston in support of the nurses's strike which had paralyzed the city. The National Guard had been sent in to deal with the trouble; a curfew had been imposed every night. When I was half-crazy for pigs' feet, John-Paul said we just had time to drive over to America Street to buy some. We never made it, being chased by a bunch of red-faced guards screaming obscenities from their truck.

Right into our private driveway they followed, ripping up a crape myrtle, arresting us both at bayonet point. I thought of Nazi Germany. Then off we were carted to the city jail. As they hustled me upstairs, the last I saw of John-Paul he was beaten up; his face and hands were cov-ered with blood.

They locked me in a cell, and what a revelation it was. Roaches crawled like small armies up walls and over ceilings. As my jailers had taken my shoes because they had laces, I jumped on top of the cot to escape the vermin.

About to panic, I thought of Mother Rutherford. What would that indomitable Miss Marple-like presence have done? "Keep calm. Think hard."

Then I remembered that I had read somewhere how a prisoner by law is allowed one telephone call. I shouted at the top of my lungs until two of Charleston's finest came flying to the door.

"I wish to call my lawyer. I believe that's my right." Even they had to agree that it was. I called Brantley Seymour who came at once, a coat over his pajamas, and still in his slippers, to bail us both out.

Next day the magistrate dismissed the charges. The courtroom was packed. When we left hand-in-hand, black men of all ages, in a noble gesture from the heart, threw down their jackets for us to walk over.

There also was to be another birth of sorts, the first book published under my married name, Dawn Langley Simmons, which I've used professionally ever since. It was a biography of that most maligned of American first ladies, Mary Todd Lincoln, appropriately called, *A Rose for Mrs. Lincoln*. As Lincoln buffs have eyes in the backs of their heads, it was a bit presumptuous for a Britisher to write it. However, as Abraham Lincoln had freed John-Paul's ancestors, it seemed more than appropriate. Besides, it was dedicated to him as my personal wedding gift. Unfortunately, it made little money and for a good reason, even though the critical reviews were some of my best. The publisher, Beacon Press, Boston, had apologized, telling me that money that should have been spent on advertising my book had gone in lawyers' fees fighting the Kennedy family. They had just published the first book on Sen. Edward Kennedy's sad role in the mysterious drowning of Mary Jo Kopechne.

There was little time to dwell on the Lincoln book's fate for it was necessary to make a quick visit to England for personal reasons. First to see Mother Rutherford, fast failing although Father Stringer insisted she was improving; and, secondly, to be examined by my Harley Street gynecologist whom I trusted implicitly. Miraculously, in spite of all the worry I'd been through while losing my house, I was not in bad shape.

I wish I could have felt the same about Mother who had aged terribly in the short while since our Hastings wedding. Michael Noakes had just painted her portrait, that now hangs in the vestibule of London's Globe Theatre, together with the almost Holbein-like drawing of her for the National Gallery. The artist was surprised that she seemed so much smaller than on stage or film.

Mr. Noakes remembers, "She had a tranquility by the time that I knew her. When I showed them the pictures after I had completed them, for I do not like people seeing my work before that point, Stringer—with all the amazingly rich and exciting things that had happened in their lives to draw on—bubbled with excitement and said it was the happiest day of his life. Perhaps it was 'our lives.' It could not possibly have been remotely true, but it was so modest I thought at the time he believed it!"

I am sure that he did believe it, having a childhood quality about such things that could only be matched by Mother. It was easy to believe that in proposing marriage he had actually knelt on one knee.

Although I did not realize it at the time, that would be my last happy visit to Elm Close. Three things remain fresh in my mind. First, Father taking me to a little dress shop in Gerrard's Cross village where he chose a pretty blue tea gown for me. Secondly, a bacon-and-eggs supper at which Mother wore a blue mop cap that was straight out of the early 19th century. The kitchen windows were wide open, for the British love their fresh air. She must have noticed my lack of ease for I kept turning my head to look into the garden.

"What is the matter?" she said.

Automatically came the answer, "I'm afraid of being shot."

There was a deep silence, then Father exclaimed, "Margaret, *Watch on the Rhine*. It's just like that scene in *Watch on the Rhine*." Then he explained that in the film of the Lillian Hellman play came the moment of truth when Bette Davis's American family finally realized how her husband, played by Paul Lukas, has suffered at the hands of his Nazi persecutors. Father and Mother were both of the theater, seeing the world of truth through the eyes of an actress. They knew I had meant it—I was afraid of being shot.

The third memory was of a Sunday evening as Mother and I sat in the inglenook while Father puttered in his beloved kitchen. I believe she was more realistic than Father, knowing how her days were numbered, that she was quietly slipping away from us. She must have felt that she would never see me again in this life. She picked up a slim volume of poetry by Mary Wilson, wife of Prime Minister Harold Wilson.

"I'm going to read you my favorite," she said, looking me straight in the face, "and I want you to remember the words always. Then, my dear Pepita (for she always called me by my second name), you will never be lonely."

In that lovely voice which had delighted so many in the past, just for my ears alone she began:

> *If I must die, as die I must*
> *First let me fully live.*
> *And grasp and hold a thousand joys,*
> *and take as well as give.*
> *And let me no experience miss*
> *But taste and savor all,*
> *And dance throughout the dazzling day*
> *On which the dark will fall.*
> *And may the pattern of my life*
> *Lie strand on scarlet strand*
> *'Til God leans from his sapphire throne—*
> *The hour-glass in His hand.*

It was dark and the street lamps were lit when they stood at the front door to bid me goodbye, Mother wearing one of her magnificent capes.

I returned to an empty house. John-Paul was down in the projects where he now spent much of his time with his son, "The Little Prince," as the neighbors had dubbed him.

Since age 12, I had supported myself with my writing, first in the Sussex newspapers at home, then later with my books. I was represented by two agents, one in London, who had introduced me to the other in New York. Financially, they had prospered with me. I thought they were my friends until I received a "Dear John" letter from the woman in London followed by one from the man in New York, who weakly deferred to the wishes of his London counterpart because she had made our initial introduction, recommending me as a client. It didn't take long to find out the real reason; the American woman with whom the English woman had lived for years didn't like black men. It was just another racist act.

Good agents are not easy to find. When I most needed my American agent, he deserted me. Lack of proper professional representation made future literary properties harder to sell.

As the months passed and the time for the baby's delivery came closer, I found it hard to walk downtown. Money was in short supply, as John-Paul didn't work. His idea of my support was a sink full of floating dead fish that he had caught that morning in Colonial Lake. By selling off my jewelry downtown, a piece at a time, I could treat myself to nourishing food.

One hot summer morning, as only Charleston mornings can be hot, I was on my way downtown on just such a mission, when my swollen ankles gave out and I sank down on a grass ledge by the side of the road. At that same moment a door opened opposite and a little wrinkled black woman walked out onto her porch where she spotted me.

"Child," she asked kindly, "are you hungry?"

"Yes," I truthfully replied.

"Come in."

Then Grandmama—her name was really Evelyn Bernell—threw her old arms around me and guided me into her spotless large kitchen. Years later, when filming her for a New York documentary, Dena Crane said, "Grandmama is surely the true definition of a *real* Southern lady."

A week before my child was born I received a visit from Cousin Alexis, together with my Aunty Babs Burgess, the most romantic of my relatives. Carefree and single, between one of her marriages, Cousin Alexis was resplendent in shimmering white.

"Summer mourning," she explained, though I wasn't aware that any kinsfolk had passed on. She was driving a cream-colored sports car and wearing a large floppy lace hat to match.

"We are going on a picnic, dearest Cousin," she said. Her whole idea of a picnic was champagne on the Battery. As one glass of champagne is my limit, and she kept pouring me more, it's a wonder that the poor child wasn't born in her car!

Far from the turmoil that had been our Charleston experience, our second daughter was born in a Philadelphia hospital, October 15, 1971, my birthday. In Charleston, I felt I was surrounded by enemies. Here, two British cousins were in attendance while two other cousins, Nigel and Maureen Burgess, promised to look after this precious gift should anything happen to me. The Lord had marked her as ours with chestnut hair like mine and the family mole on her left foot, a legacy from Caroline Combridge Hall, the pioneer woman farmer who gave birth to my great-grandfather, Alfred, in the year 1836. Margie had joked about those moles in a letter written just before she left us. "That Caroline Hall and her moles. I do think that mine is fading." The new baby was the sixth generation to have one.

When I arrived back in Charleston, October 20, it was pouring rain as they wheeled me to a taxi outside the airport. It was West Grant, the hairdresser, now my friend and neighbor, who met me and took me home. It felt cold and clammy as he turned on the gas fire. John-Paul was nowhere to be seen. When at last he surfaced he was feeling no pain, as a photograph taken with the new baby clearly shows.

"Whoever saw a blue-eyed nigger?" he asked in amazement.

"All babies' eyes are blue," I ventured to tell him. They soon turned brown with flecks of green, just like Margie's and mine. Then, as her skin seemed flushed, he started calling her "Red."

At Little Shiloh, as I called it, the A.M.E. Church whose members had been so kind to me, the baby, wearing a long white family gown, was named Natasha Marginell Manigault Simmons. West Grant had chosen Natasha, meaning white anemone, I was told, after we had seen the Russian-set movie, War and Peace. Expecting Natasha to have been a boy, Jeremy Paul was the name I had chosen. But as we left the theater West asked, "What if Jeremy turns out to be a girl?" Marginell was a combination of my three mothers, Margie, Margaret and Nell. As Margie's school friend, Gerty Baker Lysaght Dunstall said at the time, "You remembered them all."

Although John-Paul spent most of his time with his son and old love in the projects, I was as happy and content with our own baby as any new mother could be. John-Paul's mother said, "What does she know about babies?" But, I followed the directions of my pediatrician, Dr. Allen L. Harrell, to the letter. He was located beyond the city limits, so either West or a Christian white lady, Florence Haskell, drove us for regular appointments in their cars. We could no longer afford a car of our own.

Fortunately, I had Grandmama Bernell and her daughter, Rosabelle, who became one of Natasha's godmothers. They called her "Wee Baby." After raising many of Charleston's society babies, Grandmama would last care for Natasha. How she loved that little child, singing her wonderful old songs like "The Old Brown Donkey" that she herself had learned as a child on Edisto. While John-Paul was always calling home for cash to take his son to the hospital emergency room, Natasha never had to go once. The only time she was sick was for two or three days while teething. With Grandmama's expertise, I grew to know plenty about raising babies.

Sadly, peace of mind was not mine for long. First, there were the kidnap notes crudely written in pencil and poked under my front door. The police, never any help to Dawn Langley Simmons, took no notice. They all blamed John-Paul, and he played into their hands. If he had only stayed home when we needed him, he would not have fueled their suspicions. All this upset me so much I thought I would crack, so I flew with Natasha to New York where I recharged my batteries, staying in a hotel where old friends could visit me. I sold Isabel's silver necklace to pay for the three-day trip.

Miss Jackie, my faithful German shepherd who was well known to the hundreds of tourists who had visited my Society Street home, had become much attached to the new baby as from puppyhood she had always been to me. A night or two after our return home I heard a scuffle downstairs and went down to find the back door kicked in and Miss Jackie, my faithful companion, lying dead on the kitchen floor, a bloodied wooden bat beside her. It was horrible. I had loved Miss Jackie so much.

Still, there was some comfort in Margie's written declaration, "If there are no dogs in heaven then I will stay outside in the kennels."

As an act of compassion, long after we had left Thomas Street, the new owner, Alice Conroy Marks, allowed me to return for Jackie's ashes. Jackie's portrait, greeting visitors to the lost 56 Society Street house, now hangs in my home in Hudson, New York. As befits a Charleston-born pedigreed dog, the artist has the Flag of the Confederacy proudly flying in the background.

As John-Paul discovered the hard way, nobody wants you when your money runs out. He had no car anymore to taxi "friends" and family around. He had worn it out. In addition, I had our own child to feed and support without providing for somebody else's. He had promised to buy Natasha a Christmas tree (she was then three months old). When Christmas Eve came and the tree still hadn't made an appearance, it was obvious he wouldn't appear either. Matters were made worse when Mr. James, who periodically came to check upon "old Missus," told us there were more colored lights on a certain house than all the others in the projects. When he had gone, I asked Rosabelle's 12-year-old daughter, Annette Waite, to accompany me to see if we could still find a tree. We did, a little artificial one all frosted in white. Decorated with silver tinsel and bright colored balls, we later took pictures of baby in front of it. Natasha spent her first Christmas at Grandmama's house. In spite of John-Paul's absence for that season of the Christ Child, I felt richly blessed.

Then, in the early hours of Christmas morning, John-Paul came home so visibly upset I thought he'd been drinking. Thinking back now I feel it was the first of the rages that would rob him of his sanity.

Switching on the light and waking me from a sound sleep, he announced in a loud voice that he was going to fetch his son and give him to me, that I would then bring up Barry with his stepsister. I was very fond of the little boy, who had been to our home to see the new baby. But common sense told me that no mother as devoted as Dottie was going to hand her child over, even to his distraught natural father, at four in the morning!

"John-Paul," I reasoned, "you can't get that baby in the middle of the night. Wait until daylight or somebody will be hurt."

Ironically, that somebody was me.

"You don't want my child," he suddenly screamed, grabbing my shoulders, shaking me hard then pressing my throat. John-Paul weighed nearly 200 pounds. He was strong. I knew I was choking. My husband was killing me. As life ebbed away, an amazing thing happened. I seemed to be floating above them. John-Paul, the great rage having passed, suddenly realized what he was doing, an event that would recur time and again in the years that followed. His hands dropped limply from my throat. He placed my head, dripping blood from the mouth, gently back on the pillow. Nearby, Natasha blissfully slept in her little blue cradle. It was all so uncanny. I could see everything. I was looking down at them.

"Oh, my God!" John-Paul said. "I've killed my wife." Jumping up, he picked up our child, then laid her beside me. Going over to the gas wall heater he turned on the gas, not troubling to light it. Then lying down on the other side of the baby, he whispered, "When we wake up we'll be together in heaven."

"John-Paul," I spoke his name as, with super-human effort, I propelled myself back into my body. "John-Paul, I'm not dead. Turn off the gas."

I have reports of other cases where others near death, or already thought to be dead, have had the same experience. John-Paul was a strong man with fingers like steel. It is hard to believe how a woman, 5'6" and weighing 103 pounds could have survived.

To his credit he ran to find Grandmama and Rosabelle, who took the situation calmly in hand. Although they never forgave him, they did their best to help him save face, washing the bloodstained bedclothes and my nightgown. As Rosabelle said, this was all the police were waiting for, but this was one time they would never find out.

In England, things were also chaotic. My adoptive parents were in sad financial difficulties. I sold my Washington Allston painting to the Museum of Early Southern Decorative Arts in Winston-Salem, North Carolina, to help them, but it was not nearly enough. Elm Close was sold to an Arab family who later invited Natasha to play on their new lawn. As Father Stringer said, with a sense of resignation, "Well, they *did* put up a nice gate."

They bought a bungalow a few miles away at Chalfont St. Peter that was far too small for all their belongings. The Oscar Mother had won as best supporting actress for her role in *The V.I.P.s* now stood proudly on the small sitting room mantelpiece. Father afterward said how kind their new neighbors, particularly the children, were to them in their new home, as he pushed Mother around in a wheelchair. One of his letters told how he had engaged "two lesbian nurses" who would lift Mother bodily into their car, then take her for a ride through her beloved Buckinghamshire countryside.

Mother's last message to me was "One day you will go home to Charleston where I hope our grandchild will become a leader among her father's people." I still hope so, too.

They still had their "moments" for Mother's multitude of fans did not forsake her. "Dear Lady," wrote Jan van Lindt, a Dutchman of 48, "I remember one of your nice films in which you said to the tulips and birds, 'Good morning.' "

Once when she was in the hospital, Prime Minister Edward Heath visited her. Fellow-actress, Dame Flora Robson, described the visit to me in a letter: "She was so generous with her money. She was running short. Heath took her £2,000 from the Civil List, which is only given to those who have done a great deal for the community."

Father was confused by nursing regulations and wrote me complaining about his frustrations: "Although the physical side of your mother's recovery seems to be slow but sure, mentally and psychologically we have both had much to stand up to. I have been driven nearly crazy by *nobody telling me anything* and my doctor never getting in touch with me. At last I declared *near war*! This had come to a *head* and, this morning, I am actually granted an appointment with the doctor and Margaret together."

He was upset that more people didn't visit her. After the frightful picture of Mother struggling to talk with the Prime Minister that appeared in the press many thought it more kind to stay away. However, one old friend who had shared some of her stage and screen triumphs did not desert her. Dear faithful Robert Morley wrote me: "My last visit to Margaret's bedside was shortly before her death when she was strangely troubled and unhappy and naturally didn't have any idea who I was. She had an unhappy last few weeks, but a very happy and filled life before that. She was for a long time the safest box office bet in the business and she knew it, the dear old bird."

Early on May 22, 1972, West Grant, worried that I would first read it in the morning newspaper, came to tell me he had heard on the radio that Mother Rutherford had died. She was 80. Messages poured in from all around the world to both Father and me including one from Her Majesty the Queen. More than 3,000 letters were delivered by mail to my broken down Thomas Street home.

As Natasha's name was not yet added to my passport, I decided it best to go home and comfort Father when all the excitement was over. Once more I sought the sanctuary of friendly Little Shiloh. There, wearing a simple black dress with Natasha lying asleep on the pew beside me, I read through the Church of England's "Burial of the Dead." I was very comforted.

A Mostly Pleasing Interlude

"The Down are sheep, the Weald is corn, You be glad you are Sussex born!"

Rudyard Kipling

F ather cabled, "Come at once. Urgent." As the message arrived the same day as my amended passport, John-Paul agreed that the baby and I should go. He had genuinely liked my parents. Besides, while we were in England Tom Savins had promised to baptize Natasha in our own Anglican liturgy.

I carefully packed the small, white silk dress that Bette Davis had given her. I'd admired it once in a photograph. It was the dress her own daughter, B.D., had worn to her christening. Bette, when it was my time, remembered and sent it to me. Florence Haskell gave me a Charleston bonnet to match.

Natasha was the sort of outgoing baby who created attention everywhere. The Charleston airport was no exception. While I had my tickets checked, Gen. Mark Clark and Mrs. Clark asked if they might hold her. Gen. Clark, president of the Citadel, was always kind to me and years later, recalling the incident, sent me an amusing anecdote for a book I was currently writing. It seemed that his daughter had once brought home a handsome young actor named Ronald Reagan as her date!

There were two letters waiting for me at the hotel in London, one from author Gwen Robyns and the other in a grubby envelope addressed childishly in pencil. I opened Gwen's first.

In it she welcomed me home to England, then said that she thought I should be aware of what had happened in the new bungalow at Chalfont St. Peter since Mother's death two months before. To say the least, her news came as a shock to me. Father Stringer was in an awful state of mind, crying at intervals, on and off. Yet, in the midst of all the confusion, he had become engaged to marry his housekeeper.

I had heard briefly of this lady in one of his letters. He had engaged her to look after them before Mother's final hospitalization. She had once been an opera singer. According to Father, she had been desperate to find a home for herself and her cat.

The second letter was postmarked Chalfont St. Peter and was unsigned. Badly punctuated and with many misspellings, it advised me to go back to America, that "Mr. Davis doesn't want to see you or your coonskinned baby."

Somebody obviously didn't want me to visit the bungalow. Nevertheless, next morning I set out on the train for Gerrard's Cross station. It was midday by the time I arrived to be met by our old driver, Mrs. Jones, in her peaked chauffeur's cap. She had taken Mother and Father to Hastings for my English wedding.

"Thank goodness, you're here," she greeted me. "Things are bad up there. Poor Mr. Davis keeps crying. He's met three trains already this morning to see if you'd come."

This hardly sounded like somebody who didn't want to see me.

"Who is this housekeeper?" I asked as we drove up the hill towards Chalfont St. Peter.

"Housekeeper! I don't think she ever kept house in her life. Poor Mr. Davis, he's not well...and that woman seems to have taken over."

When we arrived, Father met us at the door. He kissed me profusely, then carried my big baby. His eyes, always his best feature, were puffy and red. He had aged terribly since the last time I saw him. Always neat in appearance, his shirt cuffs were soiled and frayed, his trousers unpressed, a caricature of the debonair actor he always had been.

Then I saw his housekeeper, or fiancée, as she saw fit to introduce herself. She was a large lady of uncertain years with bright red hair, clothed in nothing but a dirty white terry cloth wrapper; even her bare feet needed washing. She sat astride our family piano stool as if she were riding a horse. The voluptuous fiancée left little to the imagination. Mrs. Jones gulped as she brought my luggage. I could read her thoughts as she bid us goodbye.

"What would your poor mother have said?"

Father said he would show his granddaughter the wild birds in the garden. Mother once said, "When Tuft (as she called him) goes to heaven all the birds from Gerrard's Cross will fly out to greet him."

I handed him Natasha, who had the friendliest nature, then watched as they disappeared through the French doors. There was no time to be lost. As the old saying goes, "The show is not over until the fat lady sings," and this one was going to *sing*.

"There was an anonymous letter awaiting us at the hotel," I began. "Somebody did not want me to visit my father. I have sent it to Scotland Yard. After all, Mother's cousin Tony Benn is a member of Parliament. We have always respected the law."

She turned a purplish crimson.

"You sent it to Scotland Yard!" Guilt was written all over her face. "I wonder who could have sent it?"

Then, quickly, father's housekeeper-cum-fiancée changed the subject.

"Do you like cats? I hope one day to start a home for cats in Wales." She might have said more, but at that moment Father returned with Natasha.

"The birds must be on holiday. See what she has brought you." Natasha was clutching a flower.

Mrs. Jones was due back in an hour to take us to Gerrard's Cross churchyard so that I might see where Mother was buried. In the meantime, Father asked my advice on the disposition of the capes she had worn in the popular Miss Marple movies together with the hat she had worn to Buckingham Palace.

It was decided that one of the pale green capes should go to the costume collection at the Victoria and Albert Museum, the small blue hat with another cape to the Theatre Museum, Booth Bay, Maine, whose curator, Franklyn Lenthall, was one of Natasha's godfathers. We were kneeling on the floor packing the items when I chanced to look up at the mantelpiece upon which the Oscar statuette, the Companion of Honor insignia and other awards were all cluttered together. The Companion stood out in my memory. It would later disappear.

As we were finishing our packing the efficient Mrs. Jones came bustling in. "Well, you look better already, Mr. Davis," she said. "Maybe Dawn should take you back to America."

As we left for the churchyard, the red-haired fiancée began playing the piano; then as suddenly she burst into song.

"I do wish that woman would shut up," Father grumbled. "She sings Blake's *Jerusalem* in the middle of the night."

Father had Mother buried under the spreading branches of a large blue spruce around which the graves were arranged like the hands of a clock. The parish church of St. James, Gerrard's Cross, stood like a backdrop. The grave had to sink before the pink granite headstone could be placed over it.

"I have chosen for the epitaph, *A Blithe Spirit*," he told me. Then, as if an afterthought, he added, "It will be another place of pilgrimage when the Americans come."

We looked at the grave, gay with blue lobelia and small pink begonias, he holding the baby.

Then his face clouded over. "I don't understand what is happening. I've been so very upset. I've shed waterfalls of tears for Margaret. That woman came to help, but refuses to leave. She tells people she will marry me, but my dear, there are things I couldn't do with her that I could with your mother."

"Go back to work," I suggested. "You are a very good actor. That would help get your mind back together. Isn't that what Mother would have wished?" He nodded in agreement.

"Dawn Pepita, I have something to tell you. A burden perhaps, but you are a writer. Perhaps you can tell the world in a way that is kind."

Then, by the grave, he told me the true story of William Rutherford Benn, Mother's unfortunate father.

After her mother committed suicide by hanging herself from a tree in India (she had been lonely and sick, suffering from mental depression), her father, William Rutherford Benn, brought little Margaret home to be raised by her spinster Aunt Bessie Nicholson in Berkeley Place, Wimbledon, who, like the rest of the family, led the child to believe that her father was dead.

She was 13 years old when an old tramp came to the door and told her, "I have brought you a message from your father."

"My father? My father is dead. He died in India nursing the sick when I was a baby."

The old tramp shook his head. "Your father's shut up in Broadmoor."

Broadmoor was where they sent the criminally insane. What had he done to be sent to that terrible place?

"He..." Father paused, "...killed his clergyman father. He was mentally sick, prone to violent outbursts. The Benn family forgave him for they knew he was a very sick man. His sister always slept with his picture by her bed. Poor man, he was quite insane."

I thought of John-Paul and his violent outbursts, of his mother's schizophrenia, then back to Mother, recalling small incidents that now fitted together like the parts of a jigsaw puzzle. All her life she had been fascinated with prisons, reading to the inmates on Sunday afternoons. How she had longed to portray Elizabeth Fry, the great prison reformer. We were hard pressed to persuade her to take the detective Miss Marple's role in *Murder She Said*. Sitting over tea in the garden at Elm Close the word *murder* seemed anathema!

The Rev. Julius Benn, Mother's grandfather, was, by contemporary accounts, a saint to his generation as Mother Teresa is to our own. A dedicated evangelist, with his wife, he ran a mission for the homeless at the Old Gravel Meeting House in London's impoverished East End. There, according to his descendant, Tony Benn, Charles Dickens often visited him seeking local color for his novels. The Rev. Benn would show him through squalid opium dens and terrible slums. The minister was sometimes helped by one of his sons, an aspiring silk merchant, William Rutherford Benn, described at the time as being "notably generous to the needy." As for the Rev. Julius, he never walked where he could run, charging into the infamous opium establishments, scattering pipes and sinners in all directions. Remembering his Master's admonition to give worldly goods to the poor, the Rev. Benn was at times so financially embarrassed—a trait that my Mother had obviously inherited—that family members and admiring friends took up discreet collections to help him.

William, Mother's father, began to have what were loosely described as "breakdowns," falling into fits of deep depression, alternated with bouts of "unusual excitement and irritability." At one time he had to be placed in Bethnal House Insane Asylum.

Later, the Rev. Julius took his son, then to all appearances recovered, to Matlock Bridge in Derbyshire, described as a "Gothic paradise," for a holiday. It was there that the ultimate tragedy occurred when the unlucky William smashed in his father's skull with a Staffordshire china chamber pot, killing him instantly.

I carried out Father's wishes, retelling the long-forgotten Victorian tragedy when I wrote Mother's biography, *A Blithe Spirit*. Ironically, it had already appeared in one British newspaper when Rupert Murdoch, wanting to get something nasty on politician Tony Benn, had his researcher investigate his family history. Their findings backfired when they discovered that the father of beloved Margaret, a British institution, had killed his own father. Mother, though dead, still got plenty of sympathy.

Father Stringer suggested that I should go down to Sissinghurst so that my natural father, Jack Copper, could see his new grandchild. "You will never regret it," he said, and, as usual, he was right. I took Natasha down on the train, taking a taxi to Sissinghurst from Staplehurst station. Jack did not know we were coming. By then, his usefulness over, he had left the castle to live in a small cottage in Sissinghurst village, but even that was not permanent as it belonged to the National Trust. I guess I had expected too much, for the man I remembered, always robust and the picture of health, was now a poor broken man on two sticks.

He welcomed us both, taking me in his arms as he should have done many years before. Even then it was not too late, for all the hate and rejection simply fled from my heart. He was so happy with the baby and so was Laddie, his small white dog that had once been Sir Harold's and now suffered with heart trouble.

Then he showed me the letter he had received from Vita's younger son, Nigel Nicolson, at the time he said goodbye to the castle: "This, I am afraid, ends your long service to my family and to myself, and I want to thank you for all you have done for us and for Sissinghurst over these many many years. I hope you will be happy in your retirement, and that we shall see a lot of each other during the coming years."

Since Margie's death, his health had deteriorated. He kept repeating, "I do miss her so." Suffering from delayed shock, it was as if the use had suddenly gone from his legs. His grief was not so emotional as Father Stringer's. Jack's for Margie was silent, lingering. From the day they had married she had seen fit to wait on him hand and foot.

As I wanted to visit Margie's grave I asked Jack if he would like to mind the baby. I was not prepared for his answer.

"You mean you would let me?"

"Well, you *are* her grandfather," I said with a smile, and when I left them she was being bounced up and down on his knee, much to the curiosity of the poor invalid dog.

Natasha Marginell Manigault Simmons, a delight in the dress that Bette Davis had given her, was baptized by the Rev. Tom Savins in that same Hastings church where her parents had been wed. Father Stringer, mercifully without the "fiancée," arrived all smiles, clutching a silver christening cup in his hands. On an envelope he had carefully written: From The Late Dame Margaret Rutherford, O.B.E., (Order of the British Empire) followed by the message: "This is surely one day when dear Mother and Father can be with Natasha, you (Dawn) and, please God, John-Paul, in the Love of the Lord."

He never once forgot the young man he had tried so hard to teach how to succeed as a background husband.

It was a beautiful christening in such a medieval setting, friends and relatives all holding candles. Aunty Babs, Margie's sister, and her husband, Ernest Burgess, were there with all the Burgess cousins, and of course dear Elsie Carter, my grandmother's friend, together with other friends from my Heathfield youth, all happy to see me, as they thought, happy at last.

Only one person was missing and that was dear Rosy who was slipping away from us and died shortly afterwards. Her longtime friend, Walter Henshaw, who boarded with Rosy and her husband Alfred Stanton, stood proxy for her as a godparent.

Already the actress, Natasha kicked a white satin slipper right into the font! Soon we were outside, facing the cameras, church bells pealing and Father Stringer all smiles. It was really his swan song, back into the limelight.

After the reception in Eastbourne, I kissed him goodbye as he hurried off to his train. Shortly afterwards he passed away quietly in his sleep. It was as if Mother Rutherford had said, "You have gone through enough, dear heart. It's time you came back to me."

However, repercussions followed concerning Father's estate. There was no will. His fiancée/housekeeper disappeared. And, family heirlooms began turning up in antique shops all over Buckinghamshire, presumably sold by the housekeeper. This continued to happen for years. After we moved north from Charleston, the Catskill, New York police department received a message through Interpol that my silver tea service was safe in the police station at Chalfont St. Peter!

One of Mother Rutherford's most devoted American fans, Chester Page, a friend from Brooklyn Heights, alerted me to the fact that all the letters I had ever written her were being offered for sale by a Dutch manuscript dealer. Most disturbing was the press report that her treasured Companion of Honor insignia was being auctioned by one of the largest and most reputable auction houses in London. Such an uproar followed, it was hastily withdrawn. The person who had offered it for sale insisted that Mother had given it to him. As I wrote Scotland Yard, I knew this to be untrue as I had seen the insignia standing with the Oscar statuette on the mantelpiece in her bungalow the day we sorted her Miss Marple cloaks.

I did write the Queen that I knew my mother would never have parted with it, and a letter came back from a lady-in-waiting that the Queen agreed and fully understood what had happened. Mother always did say that Her Majesty was a very compassionate woman.

Sadness And Madness

"Sticks and stones may break my bones but words can never hurt me."

Old English Proverb

B ack in Charleston I began to get on my feet again. All my life, thanks to Aunty Doom, I had developed an expert knowledge of antiques and good paintings. In this capacity I agreed to help a man from Georgia acquire a collection of fine art. He paid me generous commissions. It was a pleasant arrangement. I'd put the baby in her carriage and away we would go to track down a new work of art. In spite of all that had happened, I still had many intellectual friends in the city. After all, even the antique dealers agreed that "If it's Dawn's, it's good."

John-Paul now left us alone for days at a time. We moved from Thomas Street into an interesting old single house at the corner of Coming and Warren streets, right opposite the cathedral that had refused to christen my child. Ironically, she took her first steps on its grounds, a mecca for wild flowers in the early spring. I was happy as I could possibly be under the circumstances, though I sorely missed Margie and Mother's letters from home. Neither had I forgotten what had happened to the poor Rev. Benn. William Rutherford's behavior made me think of my husband. The slightest thing now triggered his flash moments of violence, usually directed at me.

Terrifying was the time that I sold a miniature chest of drawers of no great value for a very good price. After all, I did have a child and a husband to support! When he suddenly returned and saw it was gone, he quickly exploded with wrath. Thank God his brother arrived in the nick of time to save me for the second time or I might well have been murdered. Just the same, the left side of my face together with my nose needed reconstructive surgery. I still bear a scar where my lip came apart.

Just as before, the outburst passed quickly, bringing mortification for what he had done. Once more Grandmama and Rosabelle covered up for him.

"Wee baby's daddy can't go to prison however much we hate him."

So John-Paul stayed home to nurse me while Grandmama cared for her last baby. Then, as I grew stronger, his thoughts strayed back to Dottie and Barry, their son. He left the same day I received a sad phone call from England. Dear Jack, Vita Sackville-West's own "wicked old Copper," was dead.

This time Natasha and I flew to England via Atlanta. This was one funeral, unlike Margie's, I was determined to attend though I did feel a bit like the Duchess of Windsor when I arrived in the morning coach at Sissinghurst Church.

Uncle Thomas Snell and his wife, Aunt Emily Louisa, Jack's youngest sister, rode with me after the coffin. It was a very nice service and, what was most unusual at a Church of England funeral, the Vicar of Sissinghurst gave a short oration. "He had a very agile mind. I was pleasantly surprised when I visited him."

I thought back to all the prizes Jack had won in Burwash Sunday School for his biblical knowledge, of his interest in politics and his own Labor party. In many ways he had been a most unusual man.

His body was carried into the cemetery to be placed in a grave next to Margie's. With her wicked sense of humor she would have exploded with laughter when Aunt Emily Louisa tripped, throwing a bouquet into the grave, grabbing at my arm so we both nearly fell in. Looking back, I think Jack would have laughed, too.

There was little time to mourn the dead, for back in Charleston the forces of evil were mustering for one last diabolical thrust to destroy me for having dared to marry a black man. The most traumatic night of my life was about to begin.

Suellen Austin, a prominent local antique dealer and a very caring person, had warned me to leave town, "For they are going to kill you." Frankly, I didn't take her seriously.

"Why?" I asked. "It just isn't logical. They have stolen my home. I'm living quietly on Coming Street not bothering anybody."

How right Suellen was I would soon find out! Alone in the house at about 10 in the evening, filling a bottle for the baby, I heard a loud crash upstairs. Alarmed that Natasha had fallen out of her cot and was injured, I rushed upstairs to find out. My heart missed a beat at the door. For there, holding a knife over Natasha, was a young white man I had never seen before. He sprang towards me and twisted my left arm so hard that he left it hanging. He broke two of my toes and my nose, then brutally raped me before dragging my limp body to the second floor piazza. Picking me up bodily, he dumped me over the side.

I must have blacked out. Regaining consciousness, my first thoughts were of the baby. Crawling round to the front door I managed to get up the steps, the front door wide open yet nothing in the dining room beyond seemed to be taken. I managed to navigate the staircase, how I don't know, expecting the worst after seeing that dagger of a knife. Thank God, Natasha was blissfully sleeping, unaware of the drama so recently played. Then I looked at my left arm, still hanging limply. It was so badly broken, I was crippled for life.

I have never spoken publicly of the rape before. It was all too horrible, a nightmare that repeated itself on sleepless nights down through the years. Like a terrible secret shared only with God, it has been my personal purgatory. At different times both the men in my life betrayed my love, and an unknown assailant saw fit to defile me.

Over the years some interesting facts emerged from this near encounter with death. I had always believed that my assailant entered through a rickety old door leading up from the basement, but this was not so. Many years later, a neighbor told me that she saw a man climbing a drainpipe leading up to my bedroom piazza, that she had called the police immediately, but that strangely there was no response for an hour!

"Why?" asked my distressed neighbor. "Tell me, why didn't they come?"

Then an article appeared in *Esquire* magazine written by Albert Goldman, author of the controversial Elvis Presley and John Lennon biographies. In it, he interviewed a local newspaper reporter who had been at my first wedding and told him that I had two Chihuahuas for bridesmaids!

I was furious. Calling my media agent, Dena Crane, in New York I told her to call Albert and tell him that if he didn't retract the scurrilous story I would sue him for a million dollars.

Phoning Dena, he said if I didn't sue him she could make a video in which he would tell Dawn who really tried to kill her. Dena agreed and in the subsequent video he explained he had been in Charleston investigating close links between drug trafficking and the Mafia. He said whoever had tried to have me rubbed out like a gangster had made a contract with mobsters!

Actually, the two family Chihuahuas *were* carried downstairs on a white satin cushion, but not for my wedding. Mary Ann, the maid, asked if she might be wed in my house. My only concern was not to upset Charleston society again as I had over paying the cook's Social Security. This time I determined to ask the opinion of an impeccable source, Mrs. Mary Pringle Hamilton Manigault.

Miss Mary told me that back on their family plantation, house servants sometimes claimed the right to be wed at the foot of the stairs, and that is just what happened with my Mary Ann when she married her Mr. Porcher. It was Mary Ann who had the little dogs carried down for her wedding.

Far more bizarre was the bright sunny spring morning in 1985, shortly after Natasha and I had returned from New York to Charleston for a few months. A young man from Tradd Street rang the doorbell of 65 Warren St., a house I was renting. He had brought me a confidential message, could he please come in.

The message was stunning, for it seems his father was dying. Wanting to relieve his conscience, he thought I should know the names of the three people who had plotted my demise at the Coming Street house.

"My father and mother feel badly that they didn't do more to help you at the time, for they had often been guests in your home."

I wasn't really surprised at the name of the woman, "a terrible woman," he called her. She was a member of a prominent Charleston family and, of the two men, one should have known better. The other man met his own justice of a poetic sort, as he was, in his "respectable" middle age, arrested for sexually assaulting little children.

I thanked the young man, who then took me to lunch at Terrible Tom's in The Old City Market.

It was obvious now that I had to leave Charleston while Natasha still had a mother.

A friend from upstate New York had sent me a copy of the *Pennysaver* newspaper in which the historic Uncle Sam's house in the small village of Catskill in Greene County was listed for sale. Once the home of Samuel Wilson, the future President Martin Van Buren had been married to Hannah Hoes there on February 21, 1807. The down payment, by Charleston standards, was ridiculously small. I paid it, though I had not yet seen the house, for I was desperate now to leave Charleston. Many times since I have regretted my action. Nothing is ever gained by running away. I should have stayed and fought on.

As John-Paul refused to come with us, I gave him a truckload of furniture, including a bed and refrigerator which he led me to believe would go in a little place he had found on John's Island. Instead, he took it home to his mother. With Natasha, now a big three for her age, and the family statue of Saint Teresa of Avila, I boarded a Greyhound bus travelling North. Natasha's Chihuahua, Sam, was flown to us later. As we left the Holy City my thoughts were quite numb. Had it all been in vain, the marriage that had so shocked local society? Not quite, for I still had my own lovely Natasha.

Welcome To Catskill:
A Motel Of Horrors

"A woman, a dog and a chestnut tree; the more you beat them the better they be."

Old English Proverb

After 700 miles on the bus we arrived appropriately at Uncle Sam's house on the Fourth of July. As we reached the last hill, Catskill was spread out before us. After the glories of Charleston, what I saw was a great disappointment.

In the confusion of at last reaching our destination, tired out and hot, I left my purse containing $400 on the bus! Thank God an honest man found it; I did get it back.

Badly needing a good cup of coffee and some milk for my child, we were to discover there was not a single store open. Fortunately, we found the old Saulpaugh Hotel. Although about to be torn down and replaced by a parking lot, there we stayed that first night. Next morning, which was cool, I wheeled Natasha in her stroller to look at our new home. It was a disaster, filled with the late owner's furniture and with water available only through a hose in the yard. In my rush to find a safe haven I had bought us a white elephant.

I soon found, however, that nice people will help a woman alone with a beautiful baby. Word got around; neighbors soon pitched in to help.

Although, like the poor old Saulpaugh which had known better days, it was a nice house. Through my English eyes, a few cracks didn't matter. Rising above it was a small rocky cliff, Broomstick Hill, lost in a green mass of pine, birch and dogwood. From the sitting room window I could see Catskill Creek.

"We can be happy here," I told Natasha, "even though we have left your daddy behind."

We soon began to get the house under control. The plumbing was fixed, the kitchen stove cleaned. One man on Division Street was particularly kind to us, carrying rubbish to the dump, then painting my sitting room without charge. There is something civilized about having a sitting room. My mentor, Vita Sackville-West, thought everyone should have the luxury of his or her own.

Thank God for The Attic, a used furniture store run by Laura Romak, where one could find good pieces of furniture and occasional antiques, all reasonably priced. I soon had a bed, and Natasha a cot and highchair. My family antiques, including Chippendale and Regency sofas, Cousin Isabel's mirrors and marble-topped commodes, family paintings and other works of art had been stored with a reputable Charleston storage company until the time came I could send for them. I had brought a few small treasures with me: the family miniatures including the lovely likeness of the Condesa; her Tunbridgeware tea caddy; a small painting of my grandmother; and the historic Whitney family daguerreotypes. Natasha had carried Lillybelle, a yellow cloth rabbit that her nurse, Grandmama Bernell, had made. Sam, the Chihuahua, soon flew up from Charleston. He was so glad to see us. After all we had been through it was such peace to walk hand-in-hand with my toddler by the creek. She was always clutching a posy of wild flowers; in time I taught her their names.

Then one day our quiet lives were once more disturbed when John-Paul arrived unannounced on the bus. He had no luggage at all.

Later I discovered that there had been no little place on John's Island; instead he had moved in with his mother. When they had tired of each other he was told, "Go find your wife." He left Charleston with nothing, not even a toothbrush.

Natasha was delighted. Little girls have special bonds with their fathers. Leaving me watching from the porch they walked hand-in-hand along West Main Street picking up fallen apples on the path. Our neighbor, old Francis Yannone, the barber, invited them inside his gate, finding them a basket which all three of them filled. Perhaps he has changed, I thought, now he's away from the traumas of Charleston. Again, I was wrong.

A royalty check for $1,600 came in the mail and he watched as I opened it. When I returned from the bathroom I had no visible husband or royalty check. Apparently he cashed it by putting a small down payment on a joint tombstone for both of us. Hours later I found someone who had seen him board the bus for New York where he had an older brother living in Brooklyn.

I was relying on that money to support us, having worked hard on the typewriter to earn it. A month passed without hearing from him. Then came a menacing phone call asking for money. He wanted to come "home." For once I had good sense to put down the receiver. Next day I went to the local Department of Social Services for advice. They were very understanding. Two lady case workers returned with me to the house and were we in for a shock! There stood a barefoot John-Paul in a dirty old T-shirt and ill-fitting jeans. He walked down the steps.

"Kelly didn't want me without money. His friend drove me back."

The Catskill police later told me we were lucky, that brother Kelly was a big drug dealer in Brooklyn. Recalling that hasty phone call for more money, it made me feel sick!

It was the winter that finally defeated us. The furnace under the house thumped like a sledge hammer before finally giving up the ghost. It was the first real snowfall John-Paul had ever seen. He complained of the cold more than the baby. I had to seek help for us. It was then the local Social Services put us in the Skyline Motel, best described as a Motel of Horrors. Charleston coped with its bugs, but I had never seen roaches like these.

The manager was a minister who later did time for defrauding those same Social Services. The janitor, poor man, a much-decorated Air Force veteran, was a chronic alcoholic. The live-in lady of the evening with her three daughters, one still a child, had driven into the village with a cat and a pet rabbit some months before. Rumors said she came from an Indian reservation. One day she would vanish the same way she had come. In her youth she might have been beautiful, but that was long past. Her teeth were rotten, her behind lopsided. The minister told me she was one of life's losers so he had given her a job. We soon learned she had shot her first husband dead and had no place to go.

Rita Tuckett, the Canadian actress, once said one of my best qualities was being "naive...and don't ever lose it." Surely, sometimes I have been too naive. Such was the case with the whore at the Skyline. It was the same old story of the wife being the last to know. John-Paul was meeting her secretly. Outraged, Laura Romak at The Attic packed 16 gifts for my child that awful Christmas.

Then another woman came with her 13-year-old daughter, victims of fate, to live at the Skyline. Her name was Estella Tice Ergle, whose mother's family were those same pioneer Broncks whose house became a museum in Coxsackie, New York. Like me, Estella had lost her home, her mother had just died, and her elderly father was sick. Except for Frances, her young daughter, she was alone in the world.

The day before their arrival it had rained all day. The roof leaked badly and there was a big puddle of water in the bed they were to share. I couldn't believe that a minister of God would put two human beings in that soaking bed and I told him so.

Estella was the first to know that my husband was having an affair with our neighbor. She chanced to look through a window to see them together in bed! She was too nice to tell me.

Then one morning upon waking, John-Paul came into the room, threw the keys in my face and snatched Sam out of Natasha's little arms. He gave him to that woman's youngest daughter. I don't think that anything hurt me so much in my life.

Yet even in the midst of such an emotional upset two good things happened. I was pushing Natasha down to the village when a car stopped and a lady popped her head out of the window.

"I loved your mother. I've seen all her movies."

Then Natasha offered the stranger a bite of her apple, beginning a meaningful friendship with Mrs. Richard Tannenbaum, the local drug-gists's wife, who became Natasha's adopted Aunt Sybil.

Then there was Vita, the black and white English Springer spaniel puppy that Natasha found under her bed. How she ever got there we never found out, but according to the vet she had been drugged by her owners. Natasha came in half-carrying, half-dragging this large wooly puppy.

"Mine," she said. "Mine." After what had happened to her Sam I was determined she should keep it. When the hippies came looking for Vita, as we named her for that other dear Vita, Natasha and her friend both hid under the covers. I watched through the window as Vita's abusive owners drove off to Florida.

John-Paul and his fancy woman carried on right under my nose. I vividly recall once, struggling to push Natasha up the steep snow-covered Thompson Street hill with Vita running alongside on a leash, John-Paul sitting dummy-like beside his new love driving merrily by and ignoring us.

That Christmas I cooked dinner, inviting Estella and Frances, then I started to laugh. Estella seemed puzzled, for I'd seemed so unhappy.

"Look out of the window," I told her. She did, to see John-Paul, the woman's car engine in parts on the ground.

"He's never put a car properly together again." Although the Motel of Horrors would be condemned and pulled down, years later that old rusted car still remained on the site.

She had to buy another one from a used car dealer. Then with her daughters, John-Paul, the cat, the rabbit and the unfortunate Sam, they drove off like gypsies into the night. I soon heard through the grapevine where they were heading. He had the unmitigated gall to take them home to Charleston! There they were received by his mother who allowed them to sleep in the bed I had given her. She refused to have little Sam in the house. He died a week after, about the time my husband's mother threw them out. Moving to Folly Beach they encountered my Mr. James, who was so indignant that he spat in her face.

When Dottie heard the news of John-Paul's new love she was equally furious. When John-Paul called to visit their son she put his arm through the window, cutting it so badly he had to seek medical attention. He bears the scar to this day.

"I did it for both of us," one day she would tell me.

Estella and Frances Ergle soon left the Skyline to live in a Clark Street apartment. Luckily, I found one on Main Street over an Italian pizza house where the owners liked dogs. They forbade Natasha to run in our living room, located over their restaurant. How we looked forward to Monday, the day they were closed.

We were hardly settled when more bad news came from Charleston. All the furnishings and works of art that we had left in storage had been sold secretly at auction. Before he left, John-Paul had been going through my mail at the Skyline, looking for royalty checks. He apparently threw away a monthly storage bill and his woman signed a paper, as Mrs. Simmons, authorizing the sale of the contents in order to get some of the proceeds.

This auction had been orchestrated by an antique dealer's wife who knew just what was in some of the boxes, such as a valuable pair of Meissen urns given me by Belle Hayes, Cousin Isabel's friend, for they were marked as to contents. A woman in Atlanta later paid thousands of dollars for the urns, which the dealer had bought in a box for $7.

To this day my good friend Florence Haskell recalls how news of the sale was purposely kept from her.

"Why," she says, "I would have gone down there, bought everything, then given it back to you." Knowing Florence, a woman of her word, that's exactly what she would have done.

Even now when I visit Charleston I sometimes see my former possessions offered for sale. In early spring of 1990, walking up King Street, I spotted my Regency Hall ancestor's miniature being offered for sale.

It seems strange to tour the Charleston Museum's Joseph Manigault House and there be confronted by such loved possessions: a French harp, the Palmetto tree mirror and the Joshua Lockwood tall case clock I had bought from the Daniel Ravenel family on Broad Street. I am proud, however, that there they are safe for posterity. Life must go on. Likewise, I am pleased that I have two former portraits from my Society Street home in the Connecticut Historical Society's collection. My Rembrandt Peale portrait of Ann Hasseltine Judson, whose life story I wrote in *Gold Boats From Burma*, now hangs in Essex Institute, Salem, Massachusetts, where I feel it belongs.

On a more personal note, the dealer's grandchild was christened in Natasha's long gown—the one she had worn to her Shiloh naming. As Queen Mary said when her son, the King of England, wanted to wed Mrs. Simpson, a twice-wed American divorcee, "What a pretty kettle of fish."

Once again Natasha and I were living alone—well not quite, for we had Vita, now the most popular dog on the street. All the children loved Vita. She went with Natasha to all of their parties.

I wasn't too well. I was pregnant again. John A. Vosburgh, M.D., attended me at the Greene County Memorial Hospital. Sadly, the shock of John-Paul's desertion caused me to miscarry. Estella, who was with me, was furious.

"How I hate men," she declared. It was Dr. Vosburgh's theory that some vital ingredient was missing in John-Paul's biological makeup that caused miscarriages, for, according to Estella, his fancy woman at the Skyline had suffered one too, of which he would have been the father.

I was not entirely alone, for somebody loved me from afar. Back when Natasha and I first came to live in Uncle Sam's house, Raymond Smith had found out where we were. I had poured out my heart to him after John-Paul had arrived only to run off to Brooklyn with my royalties. He was going to rescue us when John-Paul, like yesterday's garbage, was left on our doorstep. Then when my husband ran off with his woman, Raymond decided I had to make a decision. If Mr. Simmons (he never did call him by his given name) was really out of the picture then we three would fly to Las Vegas where I would file for a quick divorce. He would then marry me and legally adopt my child.

"At least," he reasoned, "I can give you security and peace."

He was right. Unfortunately, it was not to be. Undergoing major surgery, Raymond was found to be suffering from terminal stomach cancer. I was horrified. I felt cheated by the Gods all over again. I wanted to rush to his side, but then John-Paul came back in what surely was the winter of my discontent.

Raymond's last letter to me from the hospital was simply one line, scrawled diagonally across the page.

"I long for you always."

I couldn't even leave Catskill to go to his funeral.

In my collection at Duke University is one small bundle of letters set apart from the others, tied with white ribbon. They are Raymond's. I haven't lost him entirely, for he often returns clear as day in my dreams.

"I always wanted to marry you," he always reassures me. He was the one genuine man I have had the good fortune to meet.

Like the proverbial bad penny, John-Paul always came home. We were in bed one cold snowy night when our window was pelted with small stones. The wanderer had returned, looking like a pauper, his big toes sticking clear out of his shoes. Dog-tired, John-Paul was so dirty we had to cut his clothes from him, then scrub him from head to foot while he blissfully slept. He vowed on a stack of Bibles never to leave us again. That promise lasted exactly three days, for his fancy woman returned with black plastic garbage bags of clothing tied to the top of her broken down car. Ironically, their love nest was over Estella's new apartment, which didn't please her at all. It was not long before she arrived with the disturbing news. The woman had told Estella in confidence how they planned to kidnap Natasha, then hold her for ransom. John-Paul still believed I could earn large sums of money as I had in the past.

In despair I turned to Daniel K. Lalor, my attorney, later district attorney of Greene County and now a Family Court Justice. I was in good hands, for the late Seymour Meadow, then the district attorney, was Mr. Lalor's law firm associate. Seymour and his wife Jean had been so kind to my child, letting her swim in their beautiful pool.

Dan was incensed when I told him how the woman's three daughters had pelted us with beer cans as we walked down the street, then resorted to name-calling. I remember Dan's words: "Everyone has the right to walk the streets of New York State without harassment." We went into Family Court where the judge granted me both temporary custody of Natasha and an order of protection. The nuns at St. Patrick's Academy where she was then a student were told not to let John-Paul take her from the premises. He tried, but the good sisters actually hid her in their convent.

Estella's stories became even more bizarre, for the great love above her soon turned to war. John-Paul and the fancy woman kept them awake all night with their fighting. Estella said he looked like a wild man, as if he were cracking up. That's exactly what happened. One morning the woman came screaming down to Estella, distraught offspring behind her. They had come home to find John-Paul, covered with blood like a cannibal, eating her pet rabbit!

Now John-Paul loved animals. It had been one of the things that had attracted me to him. He had to be sick. I expected the worst. He stood under my window one morning.

"Help me," he kept calling, but I was under court order not to make contact. If I had disobeyed, Natasha might have been taken away. There was nothing left now but to cry.

Estella loyally told me each latest development. Every night John-Paul went down to the now abandoned Uncle Sam's house, crawling through a window to sleep. This was confirmed when by chance we ran into him on the way back from my speaking at a women's rights meeting. He looked dirty and unkempt with his straggly beard. My heart went out to him. I was not at all afraid. Even if I had wished to, there was no way I could have kept Natasha and him from kissing each other.

The end of the sordid saga came quickly. I passed the woman in question all bloodied and eyes blackened sitting in her car in front of the jail. He had beaten her, then thrown the television in her face. It was Providence she hadn't been killed. Still ranting and raving, the police arrested him for assault. A few hours later, the woman, her daughters and their cat drove out of our lives forever. What became of them all not even Estella Ergle ever found out.

They had a bad time with John-Paul in the jail as he wouldn't keep quiet. The mental health people were called to examine him. He was, they said, mentally sick, taking him straight from his cell to the Capital District Psychiatric Center in Albany. It was the first of many such visits. The curse of chronic schizophrenia was being played out.

Doing My Best

With Natasha in school I could no longer travel to research my work—until then, mainly in the field of biography. I liked to visit places familiar to the person I was writing about. Books and magazine articles were now, more than ever, our means of support.

The *National Enquirer* asked me to visit Plains, Georgia, during the time Jimmy Carter was president-elect. As his minister had recently adopted a child of mixed heritage, I knew very well why they picked me, but we needed the money. Natasha was attending a private school in which she did not have to face the daily taunts of the friends left behind by her father's fancy woman. I taught an art class to help pay the tuition; it was not nearly enough. Although the *Enquirer* was not quite my cup of tea, its generous offer came as a blessing.

We flew down to Palm Beach where Natasha stayed with her godmother, Richia Atkinson Barloga, now divorced, while I flew on to Plains. In addition to the minister's story, I was to reap an extra bonanza. Walking through Plains I came upon an old lady selling lemonade to the tourists. As in those days the nearest motel was in Americus, some 10 miles away, she suggested I stay in her home, which I did. In the course of the next 24 hours she had introduced me both to Jimmy and Rosalyn Carter and members of their immediate family whom she had known all her life. They proved very friendly. Miss Lillian, Jimmy's mother, gave me a night-blooming cereus cactus while brother Billy was delightful, sending out to get "the English lady" tea—which turned out to be iced! I met Uncle Alton Carter, patriarch of the family, who asked me to help compile the Carters' ancestral history for the White House. Later on I wrote Rosalyns' biography as First Lady, ironically much of it dealing with her work on mental health then a book on my own courtship and marriage, *All For Love*, that was published in Britain.

If I had not had my work while Natasha was in school and John-Paul's mental condition was deteriorating, I would surely have gone to pieces. First though, there was Natasha, who reminded me of my sister, Fay, as she still does. I missed Charleston terribly, weeping silently for my lost home, sitting by the window with Natasha asleep in my lap, while snow fell mockingly on Main Street.

In time, John-Paul was sent back to us from the psychiatric center. He had boxes of pills to control his condition which he absolutely refused to take, saying there was nothing wrong with him. He would, in fact, appear perfectly normal for a few merciful weeks before signs of madness crept in. I knew only too well all the signs!

He would hear voices that only he could hear, have long conversations with "Big Girl," a three-eyed woman whom he declared lived on Mars. He would leave pots on the stove nearly causing fires, dress up like an Indian with war paint (my lipstick) smeared all over his face, parading through Catskill delighting the ignorant. It was bad enough for me to have him made fun of, and worse for a child, his ever-loyal Natasha. He would put a dress on Vita, the dog, take her for a walk, then return, forgetting where he had left her. Once when our doorbell rang in the middle of the night, I went down to find Vita in my best Sunday dress with a policeman. The kindly cop said with a wink, "I think Vita has forgotten her hat."

One Saturday he disappeared with Natasha, taking her to Albany on the bus, where he broke into a basement where he had once stayed between hospitals. With the local police hunting for him all over Catskill they blithely returned on the bus!

Unfortunate were the New York weekend home owners whose

antebellum homes sported acanthus garlands carved similar to those over our old Society Street abode. In his poor, sad mind John-Paul was firmly convinced he was home again at last. Break in a window, move in and light a fire in the grate. The horrified owners would return to be greeted by fat nude lady murals painted all over their walls. Back to the jail he would be taken in handcuffs, back to the mental hospital in a straitjacket, all the time protesting that that was *his* house.

Yet in the midst of all his ups and downs there were times of normalcy when, with Vita walking beside him, they would go gathering clay for his folk sculptures by historic Catskill Creek. At home on the kitchen table he would fashion it into "heads" as diverse as Jesus wearing a crown of thorns (a favorite subject), Abraham and Mary Lincoln, the old fishermen he had known in his Lowcountry youth, Natasha weeping tears when other children made fun of her, and always "my Langley" as he called me, sometimes with glass marbles for eyes.

One day Marna Anderson, the folk art authority, came to see us from New York, buying a head of Jesus, then arranging for seven pieces of his work, including "Black Jesus on His Crucifix" to be exhibited under the auspices of the Museum of American Folk Art. An anthropologist for the state of South Carolina, on seeing his work, later commented on how it showed clearly the continuing link between his ancestral west coast of Africa, the Lowcountry plantations, and his native city of Charleston, where sadly an exhibit of his work has never been shown.

On his now frequent trips to the mental hospital they would provide him with art materials. Then he would draw or paint in bold colors the mythical "Big Girl" who lived with her three eyes on Mars, bizarre portraits of me with green hair and Natasha with yellow. Miss Anderson likened them to the work of Sister Rosetta of New Orleans who saw visions and then painted them. She also advised me to keep folders of his work and never destroy it. When asked by Dena Crane what she thought of me, Marna Anderson replied, "I like her. She wears sensible shoes."

Another good friend from New York City was the Daily News columnist, Liz Smith, who loyally stood by me. Not a single Christmas passed through Natasha's childhood that Liz neglected sending that child a gift. When the teenage years came Liz sent her casefuls of cosmetics.

I needed such friends, for John-Paul's mental condition at times made me quite helpless. I soon learned that the mentally ill were the lepers of society, that their unfortunate families suffered as well. One night during a seizure, John-Paul pushed in my front door and the next thing I knew a summons arrived ordering my appearance in the village court, presided over by Judge Francis MacDonald. My landlord berated "her black bastard husband." The judge ruled in his favor, giving me notice of eviction. It was ironic, I thought, that my husband's people had been in America for some 200 years while the landlord, a recent arrival, couldn't even speak proper English!

We moved further down the street to a much nicer apartment while my good friend, Estella Ergle rented the one underneath. Then, one snowy Christmas Eve, my life and Natasha's took a turn for the better.

The local Presbyterian Church gave a turkey supper for the lonely, an annual event for which we were only too well qualified. John-Paul had disappeared as he now frequently did, to be found some days later walking miles away or camping in the cellar of a burned out tavern by the creek. There, at least, when he ranted and raved, no one but the birds could hear him.

Guests were already arriving when we opened the door, oblivious that a snowstorm had kept helpers away. Only one older lady in the church kitchen fixed everything, so naturally I offered to help her. By the evening's end, we had served some 50 men, women and children. The lady in the kitchen was Mrs. Howard Muller, a local bank president's widow. Aunt Adeline, as Natasha was told she might call her, was southern-born from Virginia. She would soon be appointed by New York's Governor Mario Cuomo to the Board of Visitors at the Capital District Psychiatric Center where John-Paul was now a regular patient. Not only was Aunt Adeline very understanding of our problems, she reminded me of my aunts back in England, being a good role model for my child. She made sure that Natasha went to camp each summer and attended youth meetings in the Presbyterian Church. In turn, I became secretary of its Women's Association and its unofficial historian. From being pariahs because the neighbors were afraid of my husband, we were suddenly wanted. Aunt Adeline surely saved my sanity, perhaps even our lives.

I took Natasha down to Charleston on a Greyhound bus, there being no train station in Catskill, to visit Grandmama Evelyn, her former nurse who was growing very old. When we returned, Aunt Adeline met us at the bus stop with her car, inviting us back to her house for supper. She called on the way to invite John-Paul, too. More normal than usual, he seemed overjoyed to see us, asking us to bring him back some chicken as he didn't want to go out.

Later, after we had eaten, Aunt Adeline drove us home then helped carry our bags up the two flights of stairs to the apartment. Thank God that she did, for a chaotic scene was to greet us. Broken glass lay everywhere, while buck-naked, sitting cross-legged on the floor with an axe in his hand, was John-Paul still foaming at the mouth as he screamed over and over, "I'm not going to say I'm sorry." He had demolished the furniture, the mirrors and even our child's collection of ceramic cookie jars. Once more he left in a straitjacket.

A few weeks later he returned, this time in an ambulance, his right leg strapped up in a brace.

How could anybody forget that axe or the straitjacket? The mental health people suggested he stay in a home with others like him. With the medication working, John-Paul felt better. He was determined to come home. Would I take him in? To play on my sympathy, he came in an ambulance.

With Natasha crying "Daddy," and Vita barking for joy, I was in the minority. Even the ambulance personnel gave me terrible looks. When I succumbed, allowing him in, the first thing he did was to take the support off. There was nothing at all wrong with his leg.

Dan Lalor, my attorney, now thought it best for Natasha's protection that I apply for full custody. We went into court with a report from the Social Services that I had taken John-Paul back into the home. However, Judge James J. Battisti was compassionate when he ruled, "I do not blame her for taking her own husband in from the cold." To the surprise even of my attorneys, I was granted full custody.

Then one afternoon while I was at the typewriter working on Mother Rutherford's biography, Natasha came running through the door screaming, "Mummy, the building's on fire." Smoke poured after her.

I slipped a leash on Vita, then walked her down with Natasha. Once safely outside I went back to retrieve our precious statue of Saint Teresa, Mother's biography manuscript and Lady Marjorie, my Burmese cat. On the way down, overcome by smoke, I collapsed. It was only later that I was told who had risked his own life to rescue me. It was John-Paul who had rushed in and carried me out where an ambulance took me straight to the hospital. On a lighter note, St. Teresa spent the night next door in the White Horse Tavern along with Lady Marjorie, our cat.

Peter, The Mill House And A Blithe Spirit

"Marriage, birth or buryin,'
News across the sea,
All you're sad or merry in,
You must tell the bees."

Rudyard Kipling
The Bee Boy's Song

Although the rest of the building had serious damage from the fire, with the exception of a few broken windows our apartment did not. We were soon back in residence. Every three months or so John-Paul would start talking to "Big Girl." As Natasha said, "Daddy's leaving for Mars."

It was 7 in the evening and getting dark when suddenly he turned to her and demanded in a threatening tone, "Why are you not in school?"

"I've been," she replied, going back to her homework.

"It's evening," I hastened to add.

"No, it isn't," he shouted. "Why didn't you send her?" Then he picked up his daughter, bouncing her down hard on the table. She let out a cry as I jumped to defend her, but he grabbed hold of me by the hair. Dragging us into the bedroom, he then disappeared, slamming the door and turning the key. Half scared out of our wits, we sat on the bed and clung to each other. Natasha was crying. There was one small window high up in the wall. Even standing on a chair, I still couldn't reach it. We were prisoners, locked in, not knowing if he would come back to harm us, or just leave the house and forget where we were.

As all the neighbors were afraid to come near our apartment because of John-Paul's outbursts, we could starve before anyone would know we were missing. I looked at my watch as one hour passed, and another. Then we heard the key in the lock. It turned slowly. Then there was a moment of silence. I rushed out to see my husband running downstairs.

I phoned the mental health people, as I'd done many times before. They could do nothing, they said, until John-Paul actually committed a crime! They told me to report what had happened to the police, who in turn promised to keep an eye on the building, advising us to sleep in the front room which looked down on Main Street just in case we needed to call down for help. Natasha and Vita rested better than I did, worried as usual about what had become of John-Paul. When, finally, I woke from a troubled sleep I could hear someone shouting, "Come down Mrs. Simmons. He will not harm you." I looked out of the window to see several uniformed policemen with rifles pointed up at the roof.

We came down in our robes, faithful Vita behind us. A crowd had gathered opposite by the Mayflower Café. I looked up as a familiar voice shouted, "Dawn, save me." John-Paul was clinging to a chimney stack high up on the roof.

How they got him down nobody told me. I was just told to take him clean clothes at the Greene County Jail. From there he went back to the mental institution. By this time I knew the pattern too well. A few weeks later, fortified by medication, he would be back on the doorstep. Nobody wanted him. He had not heard from his family in months. For better or worse, he was ours and we were his. In his saddened condition he had no other place to turn. Mental illness is a terrible thing.

I decided to move from that apartment of bad memories to a little mill house on Catskill Creek surrounded by mulberry trees and a small garden. A small boat could still reach our landing, for there were regular tides and an illusion of peace. For reasons best known to himself,

John-Paul refused to go with us, determined to stay in the apartment with his second Peter, an old German shepherd someone had given him. Peter, like John-Paul, had known better days. At 17 years old, he was a bundle of bones. Vita loved the ancient newcomer immediately. They were inseparable, but he was so old and feeble that even the vet thought nothing drastic could happen. He was wrong, for Vita gave birth to 14 puppies, most of whom mercifully died for she never could have fed them.

When we moved to the mill house, John-Paul, with Peter, stayed behind in the old apartment, locking the door. For nearly two weeks they never came out, in spite of the combined efforts of the police, mental health people and the Social Services who sent two women case workers who were both half frightened to death by John-Paul's behavior. He called them "old broads."

In the end, I finally got him to come out, shouting up from the street. Early next morning, the unfortunate Peter was left on the front step of the mill house while John-Paul was carted off once again.

He was away taking treatment for the next few months, which we in turn spent happily in our new country environment. For the first time, Natasha took the school bus to classes. As there was interest in Mother Rutherford's biography both in New York and in London, it seemed logical to complete it. Cousin Tony Benn was generous with family information, including a wonderful childhood snapshot of himself taken with Mother on Bexhill Beach. It would later appear in a London newspaper after publication of the book with the whimsical headline, "Who Is The Boy With The Ice Cream Cone?"

Mother was always interested in psychic phenomena, so writing her story was helped, ironically, by the eerie discovery of her Aunt Bessie's steamer trunk crammed full of old letters, documents and photographs. It happened through the strangest of circumstances when I dreamt on three consecutive nights that Father and Mother came to me; she engulfed in one of her splendid Miss Marple capes. And Father kept repeating, "The trunk is in the garage. The trunk is in the garage." On the third occasion I was screaming when Natasha, then 9, slapped my face to make me wake up.

I was so shaken and upset by my nocturnal experience that I wrote an airmail letter addressed to the present occupant of our old bungalow at Chalfont St. Peter, asking if there was anything left behind from our family's occupancy. Back came a letter saying that indeed there was "an old trunk filled with letters and photographs in the garage."

Shelley Power, then my London literary agent, hurried down to Chalfont St. Peter where she found a gold mine of information, including letters from Her Majesty the Queen, two British prime ministers, all the love letters exchanged by my parents, including his while an officer in the Second World War, a detailed motion picture contract from Orson Welles and correspondence from their fellow thespians Lord (Laurence) Olivier, Dame Sybil Thorndike, Dame Flora Robson and Charlie Chaplin. The most important data of all was the long-hidden information pertaining to Mother's father, the pathetic William Rutherford Benn.

Margaret Rutherford: A Blithe Spirit was published by McGraw-Hill in the United States and Arthur Barker, Limited, a subsidiary of Weidenfeld (Publishers) Limited in the United Kingdom.

When John-Paul was delivered back to me, this time by the police chief himself, I decided we would move across the river to the city of Hudson, where I was told that mental health patients were treated more humanely. Instead of being carted off to jail after one of their outbursts, those like John-Paul were first taken to the hospital's emergency room for an evaluation. Then they were transported straight to the Capital District Psychiatric Center in Albany, 40 miles away.

With my *Blithe Spirit* money I bought an old Federal House, more righteous than holy; but then, like the romantic I am, I always do see old houses through British and Charleston eyes.

Go And Help Lemuel!

*"Valor and Innocence
Have latterly gone hence
To certain death by certain shame
attended."*

Rudyard Kipling

With the Hudson River and the Catskill mountains as a backdrop, the city of Hudson had great appeal. It boasted period houses dating from Dutch to Victorian times, with some splendid Federal examples in between. The church bells reminded me both of Charleston and Hastings.

"We shall be happy here," I remember telling Natasha.

John-Paul's mind was now deteriorating rapidly. One day in 1986, I was summoned to meet with his doctors in Albany. They only confirmed what I had known for years, that he suffered from chronic schizophrenia, that he would never get better. The time had come, they advised, for me to commit him to a full-time mental facility. They explained how hard it was sometimes for a devoted wife to give up the reins, but that, in their opinions, it would be in the best interests of us both, to say nothing of our daughter. I was shattered. What did well-meaning doctors know of two weddings by candlelight and solemn promises made before God to take John-Paul for "my legal wedded husband, for better for worse, for richer, for poorer, *in sickness and in*

165

health?"

In addition, there was my horror of putting somebody away. The story of my grandmother's brother, Alfred, incarcerated in Hellingly Asylum for 30 long years still haunted me, and more recently, the sad story of William Rutherford Benn. I couldn't do it, it was as simple as that, so I took what I thought was the only way out. If I divorced John-Paul then Natasha would automatically become his next of kin. Being a minor she could not legally sign her father into an institution without my permission. With such a drastic step confirmed by Lance Miner, my attorney, I filed papers for divorce, but because of the serious accident John-Paul would suffer in the near future I didn't have the heart to go through with it.

Fate struck again in another recurring dream about Mother. There she was, large as life, cape billowing in the wind, clearly repeating her message: "Go and help Lemuel," she declared. "He is innocent. Go and help Lemuel!"

Once more I awoke in distress, puzzled, too, for I didn't know a Lemuel. There was a King Lemuel in the Old Testament, while another Lemuel was the hero of *Gulliver's Travels*. That afternoon in the Hudson *Register Star* a photograph seemed to leap out at me, showing Lemuel Warren Smith, a black man, on trial in Poughkeepsie for killing a woman prison guard named Donna Payant. That she was a prison guard made Mother's beyond-the-grave message more uncanny, for all her life she had been totally fascinated with prisons, inmates and guards! Hadn't she given poetry readings in the jails? As Christians we believe in life after death. By chance in the hereafter had she met the murdered corrections officer Donna Payant?

Remembering those other dreams responsible for finding the old steamer trunk, I sat down that evening and wrote a letter to Mr. Lemuel Smith.

Lemuel Smith responded. It was quite obvious that he was an articulate man. We met for the first time in the visiting area of the downstate prison facility at Fishkill, New York. Here, at least, he was not confined to one side of a long table with me on the other. The bright sunny room, set up with small individual tables, resembled a cafeteria. Although two guards were on duty, they were far enough away to allow us some privacy. After relating his story—that he was "black, poor and ugly"—the accused man told me he was innocent, that he was the scapegoat for somebody else. As an investigative reporter, I had interviewed many people, and so, feeling he was telling me the truth, left Fishkill agreeing to help him.

Donna Payant had been strangled at Green Haven Correctional Facility in 1981. Her body was found in a prison garbage landfill. At the time, Smith had been an inmate at the prison for four years and five months. He had been convicted of what were commonly known as the "Thanksgiving Eve Murders" in Albany. The murders occurred on November 24, 1976. The victims were a religious art store owner and his woman assistant.

First suspected in the murder was Payant's fellow corrections officer, Martin Rahilly, Jr., but according to the Associated Press, "As a part of a deal with the state in exchange for his testimony against Lemuel Smith, Rahilly agreed to accept disciplinary action for his admission that he was dealing drugs in the Dutchess County prison."

Smith was, in the opinion of his many supporters, simply the scapegoat. The son of an ordained minister, Lemuel Smith was convicted mainly on Rahilly's testimony. William Kunstler, the activist lawyer, valiantly defended him, but the popular press had already depicted Smith as a monster.

Once more, I visited Lemuel Smith in the prison at Fishkill. Outside, it was a warm, sunny spring day, with wild flowers everywhere. Natasha came with me. When the prisoner joined us in the waiting room, we were the only ones there. He had a great way with children, quickly forming a rapport with my daughter. We tried to be cheerful, but always the black cloud of death hung ominously over us. A week later, Lemuel Smith would be sentenced to die in "old sparky," the electric chair.

I was present at that grim sentencing. The judge looked like Woody Allen; but this was real life; it wasn't a film. Outside, marchers protested, carrying placards and wearing black arm bands, as did William

Kunstler, his lawyer. In a newscast that night, I was described as follows: "Dawn Langley Simmons, the woman activist, was present clutching her Bible." Preservationist, yes, but never before had I been called an activist.

Lemuel was transported to death row in that same Green Haven Prison, where only his elderly mother and close family members could visit him. On the outside I took up his case, aided invaluably by Dena Crane. Between us, we determined to do what we could.

First, it meant going to what I thought was the heart of the matter, the Thanksgiving Eve Murders. Going through microfilm files in the Albany Public Library, I came across a notice from the local *Times Union* offering a large reward for information leading to the murderer. Already known to be black, thought to be badly cut, the suspect had left a trail of blood from the art store to Broadway. A barmaid had seen the alleged murderer leaving the store, his injured hand hidden inside an old raincoat. She had testified that he wasn't a tall man like Smith.

Three days after the murders, Lemuel Smith was stripped down to the skin by detectives looking for knife wounds, but there wasn't a scratch on his body. And Smith told me that the blood found on the sidewalk was not the same type as his.

Lemuel sent me a report from his former parole officer stating that prior to the time of the Thanksgiving Eve Murders Lemuel Smith had been drinking coffee in the White Tower, a popular Schenectady diner some 18 miles away from the art store in downtown Albany.

Concluded the parole officer, "The police are satisfied that this is true." Lemuel said that he left the diner at 3:15 p.m. As the murders took place between 4 and 4:30, he still would have had to travel 18 miles on the bus, having no car.

Like some latter day Miss Marple, I set out with Dena Crane filming the scene with her video camera, Natasha keeping time and Barbara Streisand's cousin, Irene Carr, an antiquarian Albany bookseller, driving. I'm sure that dear Irene only drove us out of the goodness of her heart, for, like other of my friends, she could not understand why I thought Lemuel Smith innocent. However, driving back from the White Tower during what was the beginning of rush hour, it took us well over an hour. In addition, on the afternoon of the murders everyone would be hurrying home to their families for Thanksgiving. As I pointed out to the others, Lemuel would have needed wings to have reached downtown Albany so quickly, then killing two people before making his escape. Even the late Barney Fowler, *Times Union* columnist and no friend of Lemuel, in a telephone conversation with me exclaimed, when confronted with the time element, "Why that is impossible!"

The city of Hudson is like a small town. Word soon got around that I was working to prove Lemuel Smith's innocence, that in most eyes I was championing a murderer. In addition, the Hudson correctional facility provides work to many Hudson residents. Although I was following the dictates of conscience there were many others who did not view it that way. One morning on the street, I was assailed by a prison guard in uniform who warned me, "If you don't lay off the Smith case, you'll finish up just like Karen Silkwood." (Karen Silkwood died November 13, 1976, under mysterious circumstances because, it was widely believed, she "knew too much" about problems at a nuclear energy plant where she worked. She was portrayed by Meryl Streep in the movie *Silkwood*.")

This alone was very disturbing. Then Natasha came home from St. Mary's Academy in tears. The son of a city official had harassed her, screaming, "They should sit your mother in Lemuel Smith's lap and you along with them, then pull the switch."

Next morning just after eight, the front doorbell rang and there stood a young man with pad and pencil.

"Are you really going to marry Lemuel Smith?" he demanded.

I was surprised and still sleepy. My off-the-cuff reply was as stupid as his question: "He hasn't even asked me."

The young man, a reporter from the local *Register Star*, wrongfully interpreted my answer as yes. I was in shock when, that afternoon, New York Gov. Mario Cuomo's secretary issued a blunt statement: "She may wish to marry him, but she cannot. Prisoners serving life are not allowed to marry."

Actually, I couldn't marry Smith or anybody else, as I still had a husband. This did not stop truckers from screaming, "Lemuel," as I walked up the street. To add to our discomfort, John-Paul had entered a new phase of his sickness, prowling the street by night stealing smelly bags of garbage, then bringing them home.

Things came to a head just before dark one snowy afternoon. The sidewalks were so slippery that Richard Tanner, a local antiques dealer, advised me to walk home on the street instead of the sidewalk. This I was doing when I turned onto Union. It was now quite dark, and whoever hit me from behind, like the coward he was, then dragged me up onto the sidewalk. I remember clearly my assailant's red face, still in his prison guard uniform. I might well have lost my life on that deserted part of the street if a sports car had not suddenly roared to a halt, causing my attacker to flee. More surprisingly, as I later discovered, the man in the sports car was Joe Mahoney, crime reporter for the *Times Union*. He later followed the ambulance with me in it to the hospital, where X-rays showed that I had broken both my right shoulder and wrist. I was housebound for six weeks, during which time I had a good time to think. Natasha and I needed a respite from Hudson until tempers calmed down.

As for my unfortunate friend, he languished on death row for weeks, facing electrocution under one remaining section of New York's capital punishment law. Thank God, a court decision struck down that section before the authorities could kill him. Lemuel Smith, instead, received another life sentence.

According to United Press International, on November 7, 1987, Martin Rahilly, whose testimony had convicted Smith, was ordered reinstated as a prison guard: A prison guard, fired in 1983 for selling drugs to inmates, was ordered reinstated with full back pay because he testified against the murderer of fellow prison guard Donna Payant. Rahilly's lawyer Noel Tepper of Poughkeepsie said Monday "with deductions it comes to about $80,000...My understanding is he wants to return to his job at Green Haven."

My association with the Lemuel Smith case was not quite ended. Going to pick up my Sunday papers from Charley's Corner, everybody stopped talking when I walked in. I soon found out why, when I saw a pile of those supermarket tabloids with two photographs on the cover—one of Elizabeth Taylor entering a hospital to lose weight and the other of me, a most glamorous picture taken while walking down New York's Fifth Avenue to mark my engagement many years before. I didn't need my glasses to see the glaring headlines: "Actress's Daughter To Marry Triple Killer."

First thing Monday morning, I took the paper in to Lance Miner, for the story on the pending marriage of myself to Lemuel Smith was little short of ridiculous. In addition, to add insult to injury, I was supposed to have made a pornographic movie with Lemuel Smith on death row, where, not being a blood relative, I was never even allowed to visit him. The so-called movie was an innocent interview filmed by an independent television company in the courthouse at Poughkeepsie which I had agreed to do for Dena Crane in the presence of several guards and sheriffs. It was not unique, for all the local television stations were allowed equal time by the judge to make their own reports. Lemuel, in knee chains and handcuffs, was amused when I gave a bald-headed sheriff Uncle Ditcher's old gypsy raw onion remedy that made hair grow. This was as "pornographic" as it got, followed by a lot of laughter when a fellow sheriff quipped, "Don't bother telling him, Miss; there isn't anything in it." I presume he meant his head!

I Have Earned My Peace

*"As a bird that wandereth from
her nest, so is a man that
wandereth from his place."*
Proverbs 27:8

D ena Crane telephoned that the BBC wanted to include me in a special program. Alan Whicker, the Walter Cronkite of British television, was in America interviewing British expatriates. Having hardly recovered from six weeks indoors, mending my broken bones, while John-Paul had appointed himself Hudson's unofficial garbage collector, the house was in no state to receive anybody, let alone the BBC.

We extracted a promise that the filming, to be called "Whicker's World: Living with Uncle Sam," would be downstairs in the sitting room and that John-Paul's rooms upstairs, piled high with plastic garbage bags, was off limits to the crew. I was appalled when I learned that this pledge had been broken.

Dena told me that the interview might not even take place, as the BBC photographers had threatened to strike on my doorstep over some difference with Mr. Whicker.

Fortunately, peace was restored and the filming went on. I liked Jonathan Stedall, the producer, who arrived holding the most enormous bouquet of tiger lilies for me.

Although I wished Mr. Whicker had dwelt more on my achievements than misfortunes—"engaging" me to Lemuel Smith with my husband upstairs—as interviews go, it was rather enjoyable. In the course of my work I, too, had interviewed many people, so I anticipated in advance just what he would ask me.

The producer, Mr. Stedall, was fascinated with the wall full of family pictures, particularly one in which he declared I resembled Isadora Duncan, the legendary dancer. He loved the painting of Vita Sackville-West in a tri-corner hat!

The British *Radio Times*, in announcing the segment I shared with writer Pamela Kellino, actor James Mason's ex-wife, gave me a nostalgic headline: "When I Am Lonely I Dream Of Hastings."

Well, Hastings or Charleston, I love both of them equally.

There were three repercussions to the program that affected me personally: *The Kent and Sussex Courier* was surprised that Old Heathfield, my birthplace, wasn't mentioned, although I personally had no control over the interview's content; Aunty Babs Burgess in Bromley didn't like my long hairdo; and my beloved Eastbourne school friend, Pamela Pike, then Mrs. Patrick Standhaft, found me again. Pamela wrote that over the years she had followed my career with admiration but had neglected to contact me, for fear I would be too proud to remember her. Instead, it made me happy that I had a dear friend again.

Natasha was unhappy at the academy and wanted to go home to Charleston, where she had her godmother and stepbrother. John-Paul refused to go. With a monthly disability check, he could now afford a small apartment of his own. His mental health counselor in Hudson encouraged him to become self reliant. I was dubious, for I thought I knew my husband better than anybody. However, the morning he answered the front door in his birthday suit to three shocked Jehovah's Witnesses, I began to think he might be better off on his own.

He soon found an apartment on Union Street. When, at last, we said goodbye, he was watching his television from the most comfortable armchair we possessed. As Natasha explained diplomatically, "Daddy is tired of us; and we need a change." As the mental health office was a few minutes away, I knew he could get help if needed.

So it was with some relief when the furniture van drove south to Dixie in 1985. We were driven down with the faithful Vita and two puppies, Boompie and Irania. We rented a house on Warren Street, a stone's throw from the same house where I had once been so cruelly attacked. Elizabeth Hines, my former neighbor, greeted me with, "Miss Dawn, do you walk as much as you did?" Then she pointed out the large clump of mistletoe in the live oak opposite. How she had laughed one Christmas when John-Paul had found it, kissing me right there on the spot.

I found many changes in Charleston, now a city of tourists, conventions and an annual international arts extravaganza, Spoleto Festival U.S.A. The Omni Hotel complex was being built between King and Meeting streets. The popular police chief was a black man. I met bank tellers and receptionists who were black, too. At least on the surface, there were equal opportunities for all citizens. I smiled when, for the first time, I saw a young black man hand in hand with a young white woman. A black judge was living on that same Battery where John-Paul had met so much trouble when courting me. It was sometimes hard to accept all the changes I found.

Mayor Joseph P. Riley, Jr. received me quietly at City Hall where I gave him a copy of *A Blithe Spirit*, my biography of Mother Rutherford. He described a recent mayors' conference he had attended in Los Angeles, and told me that he met a group of black intellectuals, all with roots in his city. "It was quite tragic, the great minds, professional and otherwise who were lost to their native Charleston." Then he graciously apologized to me for what had happened so many years before.

"Thank you," I said. "If only you could give back my poor husband his mind." I was still bitter about what had happened to us in Charleston years before.

Then the nicest thing happened as I left City Hall. A young black woman rushed forward and held out her hand.

"But for people like you, Mrs. Simmons, I might still be mopping floors." I had always paid my staff fair wages, something that was not true of all white employers of black domestics in the 1960s.

Once more, waking up in Charleston to the sound of soft rain was a wonderful feeling. I hoped we were home for good. There's nothing quite like the river wind rustling the palmettos. Only John-Paul was missing.

Natasha was enrolled in the Cathedral School of St. John the Baptist for what was her last year before going on to high school. There she would graduate by candlelight in the Cathedral of St. John the Baptist in one of the most meaningful ceremonies I've ever attended. It was during Spoleto and, as I wrote Ashley Cooper, *The News and Courier* columnist, to hear the children sing "We Are The World" was in itself inspiring.

After my daughter left each morning for school my days were geared to a slower pace than in "Yankee-land," as Cousin Alexis, still not quite recovered from "The War," liked to call it. Now my writing was done in the evening while my daughter worked on her homework. I had started a book on the Georgia childhood of Carson McCullers, for once more, after many years, I had her close friend and confidant, Edwin Peacock, nearby. Edwin, with John Ziegler, had founded The Book Basement bookstore.

I would meander slowly down King Street to meet my daughter from school. The shoe shine man, now old and white haired, remembered me from the past, and gave me a nod. The older black ladies with their parasols; the cheery "good mornings" though in effect it was long past noon; the overall politeness of its citizens—these Charleston qualities never had changed.

When I met up with Natasha in her neat school uniform, we would make for Terrible Tom's in the Old City Market for hot sausage on a biscuit. For special treats we had supper at Reuben's on Meeting Street or a Saturday luncheon at Frieda's restaurant on Society Street. This last had a special place in our past, for when Natasha was born, Elaine Parrot the owner, gave her a carrier to travel in.

The Charleston County Library became my child's second home. She was intrigued by the computers. Researching for homework was a pleasure, not a chore. One day she read that extras were needed for the television miniseries *North and South*, a Civil War saga being filmed in the vicinity. Mother Rutherford's favorite, Elizabeth Taylor, was to play the part of a rich bordello madam. It all seemed such fun. They were asking local residents to send in their photographs for selection as extras. Unknown to me, Natasha sent in a picture of us taken together. I was shocked when it was me that they chose. She wasn't upset, for, with my crippled arm, she would be needed to help me with zippers. Everyone had such a good time, and the food was delicious! We even ate lunch in the shadow of St. Philip's, to say nothing of breakfast on the Battery where, dressed in my crimson velvet crinoline, I suddenly recalled how once I had been chased with John-Paul from that "sacred" spot.

On the bus to Fort Moultrie for filming I told Natasha that she might visit the grave of Osceola, whose biography I'd written for Holt, Rinehart and Winston. The brilliant leader of the Seminoles, he had been dishonorably captured, then imprisoned under a flag of truce. In my book, I had carefully sifted fiction from fact; no easy task, for American Indians had left no written records behind. Their avowed enemy, the white man, had written their story, often unfavorably.

In all fairness, Charlestonians had treated Osceola as a visiting celebrity, flocking over to Fort Moultrie on Sullivan's Island to see the Seminole chief decked out in his finery. He was allowed by his captors to attend a performance of *The Honeymoon*, starring the English actor, Thomas Abthorpe Cooper, and his daughter, Priscilla, in The New Charleston Theater. The audience could not foresee that the pretty actress on stage would marry Robert Tyler, eldest son of future President John Tyler on September 12, 1839. Then, because of her mother-in-law's ill health, Priscilla would fill in as First Lady.

However, on that particular evening Priscilla fancied the audience watched Osceola more than the stage. Nor was she overly pleased to be told of his preference of the trombone to her acting!

Osceola's premature death at Fort Moultrie and subsequent burial led to startling rumors that the Seminole chief had actually been buried minus his head. As my research discovered, the villain of the piece was

Dr. Frederick Weedon, the post surgeon, who had every opportunity to decapitate the chief. Embalming the ghastly object and taking it home to St. Augustine, he hung it on the bed post as a disciplinary measure when his three small sons misbehaved. Five years later he gave the once proud head to his daughter Henrietta's husband, a physician, who in turn passed it on to his own former teacher, Dr. Valentine Mott, a founder of New York's University Medical School and the Academy of Medicine.

In 1858, the Academy cataloged the exhibit in what was described as Dr. Mott's Surgical and Pathological Museum, listing: "Miscellaneous—NO. 1132 Head of Osceola, the great Seminole Chief (undoubted)."

In 1866, part of the museum was destroyed in a fire, at which time the pathetic relic was mercifully consumed.

Natasha did get to stand by Osceola's grave, watch an enactment of a Civil War battle and visit the U.S. National Park Service information center where she asked a guide a question about Osceola. She was proud when he consulted a copy of her mother's book which was hidden under the counter.

While waiting with a group of extras, I watched with amusement as a very distressed mother whose little girl was sporting a most elaborate modern hair style out of keeping with the mid-19th century, protested when the makeup lady combed it all out. The mother became belligerent when the director passed by, took one look at me in my poke bonnet and said, "Margaret Rutherford's daughter...I need you." The next thing I knew, my fellow extras were dismissed for the day while I was ordered to remain. I felt sorry for the confused little girl with the newly ruined hair as she left on the bus with her outraged mama. It would be a long day for me.

The local Stella Maris Catholic Church was being used to shoot the wedding scene of two of the principals, "Constance and George," with me, "an old Irish lady," repeating the Rosary in a pew at the back. Unfortunately, being Church of England, I didn't know the Rosary, but with Natasha's help, she having been taught in Catholic schools, I managed to improvise. The "priest" who was to "marry" the couple, played by veteran Charleston actor, William Bender, was in a similar plight, having memorized the words from an Episcopalian prayer book. We each consoled each other over our predicament.

We filmed well into the night with me repeating "Holy Mary, Mother of God" over and over again. Repetitious, it nevertheless classed as a speaking part, for which I was generously paid. Later, we shared the taxi home with the actress, Kirstie Alley, who was cradling a small pet bird in her jacket. Obviously a great animal lover, she was very friendly so the ride home passed quickly. By the time Natasha undressed me, she found my back to be bloody thanks to my tight bone corsets.

Much to my daughter's delight I was called back several times more, the most enjoyable part of which was having a private talk with Miss Alley in a room at the Dock Street Theatre. She was playing the role of a wealthy Boston abolitionist who married an escaped southern slave. As John-Paul was black and the descendant of slaves, Miss Alley was intrigued with our story. In addition, Cousin Isabel Whitney had Boston abolitionist ancestors who had known the famed Grimké sisters, Sarah and Angelica of Charleston. Members of a most prominent white family, like us, they had been forced to relocate north.

With our lives now on a more peaceful plane, although I still worried over John-Paul, our child had bonded again with her stepbrother, Barry. "Nobody will ever come between those two," declared Joannie, one of Barry's sisters. Natasha's beloved nurse, Grandmama Evelyn, was "called home" as her funeral program said, but Rosabelle, her daughter and one of Natasha's godmothers, was still living in the city. Never once did I visit Rosabelle's home that she didn't cook a delicious meal for me. As Grandmama would have said, "My child, you are home."

But black clouds were gathering. There was a most disturbing phone call from Hudson. John-Paul's landlord offered to pay my fare back to "remove John-Paul from his apartment." I begged the man to be reasonable, that I was 700 miles away with my daughter in school, explaining that all he had to do was call the mental health people for assistance. Then, I cautioned him not on any account to forcibly enter the apartment, for from past experience I knew it could only trigger violence in my sick husband. It was a replica of what had happened before on Society Street—"tearing John-Paul out of his home."

The irate landlord thought he knew better and broke in the door; John-Paul, like a madman, chased him up Union Street with a piece of lead pipe.

"That landlord ran faster than Jesse Owens," Ethel Fernandez, a neighbor, later related.

From then on it was the old story, John-Paul arrested at his apartment where his television and hi-fi were later stolen. In spite of the pleas of his mental health counselor, based on his long medical history, the landlord determined to press charges. I called on Lance Miner to defend him. Unfortunately, when Lance phoned the local sheriff he couldn't remember where he had sent my poor husband. Finally, after many long distance phone calls from Charleston, John-Paul was found to be incarcerated in an institution for the criminally insane at Rochester, New York, close to the Canadian border. It was so cruel, un-Christian and rather ridiculous.

When John-Paul was finally brought back to Hudson to stand trial, I begged both the mental health people and Lance to please ask the judge, if the case was dismissed, not just to put him out on the street with no place to go. The judge did not listen. Because of John-Paul's past mental history, the case was thrown out; but instead of ordering treatment, as in previous cases, John-Paul was set free. From Hudson, he walked the few miles to Catskill where some "kind" person gave him a one-way ticket to Charleston. Early one summer evening, after having eaten supper out, Natasha went upstairs to find her Daddy in bed.

John-Paul lasted about three days in Charleston before the effects of whatever medication he was given began to wear off. He began to feel uneasy. He begged to return to "his cabin" in Catskill. I saw the wild look in his eyes and was worried that, without the proper treatment, he would suffer a violent attack. His medical history records were all in New York State, and even my attorney couldn't get them. Somewhat apologetically, I explained to Natasha, "We have to return."

"But we've been so happy. Oh, why did he have to come back?"

To complicate matters, Boompie had two puppies. Boompie was not born for motherhood, as we soon found out. She bit one puppy, Little Margie, on the forehead, then abandoned her completely. The other puppy died. Little Margie had to be nursed with a bottle.

While John-Paul deteriorated and our daughter wept, I packed up the home and put it in storage. Vita, Boompie and Irania went into kennels while Little Margie, the abandoned pup, too weak even to whimper, traveled north with us on the train in a big zipper bag.

After an overnight journey we arrived back in Hudson. John-Paul refused to go to the mental health people for treatment, instead literally running over to Catskill.

On a Sunday afternoon, in 1987, I had an awful premonition that something was wrong. I had been to the cabin with food the previous Thursday to find John-Paul blissfully sleeping under a pine tree. It seemed cruel to wake him. By afternoon I had more feelings of impending disaster. I *had* to go to Catskill. There are no buses from Hudson to that village, and with no cash on hand for a taxi, I started to walk. A good hour later I was standing in the cabin, which was deserted; even his mattress and pillows were missing. I hurried to Main Street to be told the bad news. John-Paul had either jumped or fallen from a roof 40 feet from the ground. He had been taken to the local hospital more dead than alive. I'll never know how I got up that steep hill to his side! John-Paul had fractured his skull, broken a wrist and so badly injured one hand that it was doubtful he would ever create his folk sculptures again—and that was *if* he recovered.

Dr. William Vernon Wax told me that head surgery was necessary, that it could prove fatal, that I must sign my consent. It was a question for Solomon. Should I or should I not give permission for the life-threatening procedure? For years John-Paul's life had been sheer hell. If the Lord took him now, would he not be at peace?

I sent for Aunt Adeline who lived close by and who, in turn, fetched Natasha from Hudson. Then we explained what had to be done.

"I want Daddy to get well again," she said. Poor child, she could never remember when he had been fit and himself. So I gave my consent, kissing John-Paul goodbye as he was wheeled into surgery.

For one long week he fought for his life while we anxiously waited by his side. Then, gradually, he improved; so the day came when the doctors said he might go home. Natasha helped me get him into a taxi where, from the moment he sat down, he started to talk in a very loud voice. This went on for three days and nights until a merciful ambulance took him away.

Vita arrived back by plane that Christmas, a wreck of her former happy self, her beautiful coat mud-stained and cropped short. Boompie and Irania never returned, supposedly having died. Vita wasn't much better, with a life-threatening abscess in her ear, caused by neglect. She was taken immediately to Dr. Merrill Johnson's Animal Clinic near Hudson. Dr. Johnson was so kind to her, as was Judith Marotta, driving Vita for her now weekly visits.

Little Margie, shades of her aged, amorous grandfather, now grew into a German shepherd-type dog. She was soon joined by J.J. (short for Judith Josephine), a bassett hound, who entered our lives one Sunday morning on my way back from Christ Church Episcopal. A bunch of strange people, of Tobacco Row type, drove slowly down Warren Street in Hudson in their broken down truck. Suddenly, there was a plop and this poor, bewildered dog, little more than a puppy, was thrown at my feet. Dripping blood and milk, for she must have just given birth, J.J. looked up at me with those sad eyes that all bassett hounds have. Said an old Italian gentleman standing close by, "Mama, that poor dog needs help!"

J.J. thought the same thing, for she followed me home, then into the elevator. Little Margie welcomed her warmly.

Vita left us on Mother's Day, 1988. She walked into the kitchen, nudged me with her nose, as did Little Margie. Then she went back to her pillow, curled up and died. It was like losing a child; I was numb. Dr. Michael Marotta and his wife Judith came over to help me, while the Catskill *Daily Mail* gave Vita a proper person's obituary. Elizabeth Boice, the women's page editor, recalled Vita's popularity with all the village children from puppyhood on.

Due to some requirement in New York State's education laws, Natasha was required to attend high school for one extra year. So she chose Hudson High, with dire results. Being an exemplary child, not addicted to the current problem of drugs, I never once suspected what was going on. Then, one evening before bed, she handed me a book with the startling title, *How To Tell Your Mother If You Are A Pregnant Teenager.* It was as if a most precious vase had been shattered.

I ran like a crazy thing from the house somehow finishing up in the post office, and there he was, our assistant rector the Rev. W. Keith Hendrick, as if he were waiting. He listened as I blurted out the news of what my child had told me. Calming me down with a few kind words, he said that no good ever came out of running away. Would that I'd had that advice years earlier!

Natasha decided to keep her baby, for, as she said, "Who will adopt a black baby? The foster homes are full of them." I had to agree. Look at the classified ads in any newspaper. "Financially stable couple are looking to give a home to a white infant." Natasha's child would only be one-fourth white. The father, Sean Roberts, was, like my daughter, only 15. She had known him since they were 10. Now it would be children bringing up children.

The last weeks of her pregnancy were the worst, and while my family in England and old friends were, as always, supportive, there were some right in Hudson who were not. I remember the horror I felt when a church-going lady shouted at me on the street, "Oh, how I do wish she would fall down the stairs."

At such times I felt such a failure as a mother. If only we had not had to go back to Hudson would this tragic teenage pregnancy have happened? Had I put John-Paul's needs first in my marriage once too often? I was soon to find the answer. In Christ Church one bright Sunday morning, as our rector, the Rev. C. Robert Lewis, was celebrating Holy Communion, I chanced to look up at a stained glass window where a text leapt out at me. It was surrounded by roses. "She Hath Done What She Could."

At that moment in life I knew I would never be alone, for those were the words on dear Margie's cross in Sissinghurst Cemetery. I felt that I'd received a message from beyond the grave.

Natasha insisted I be with her in the hospital delivery room when my grandson was born. It took place early on the morning of January 16, 1988. Father Hendrick baptized him Damian Patrick Hall at Christ Church, two life-sized marble angels guarding the font. Damian is for Father Damian who had ministered to the lepers, Patrick is the second name of his father and Hall to honor our ancestral family at Withyham in England. Sean's parents have been most supportive. Damian is a dear little boy, a sacred trust, as Cousin Isabel would have said, "To carry on the family torch."

John-Paul lives in a group home for the mentally sick on the grounds of the mental hospital, where at long last he has found his own peace. I visit and clothe him. He lives in our past, which is Charleston. In his eyes, I will never grow old. The other day he asked me should he die first would I ever marry again? Once, long ago, Vita Sackville-West had asked Harold Nicolson the same question.

"No, my angel," Harold replied. "No stranger either in this world or the next shall come between you and me."

That's how I feel about John-Paul.

Together in death we will rest with Margie at Sissinghurst.

Index

INDEX

INDEX

The Author

Dawn Langley Simmons (née Gordon Langley Hall) is the author of some eighteen books including a biography of her surrogate mother, *Margaret Rutherford—A Blithe Spirit*. Her other writings include biographies of Rosalyn Carter and Mary Todd Lincoln; *Vinnie Ream—The Girl Who Sculptured Lincoln*; *William, Father of the Netherlands*; *Osceola*; and *The Sawdust Trail: A History of American Evangelism*. Her modern morality play, *Saraband for a Saint*, first performed in the chancel of St. Martin's Episcopal Church, Harlem, New York, and later published in book form, earned her an invitation to Lambeth Palace to discuss it with the Archbishop of Canterbury. She went to Plains, Georgia, to help President-elect Jimmy Carter's uncle prepare the Carter family history for the White House.

Mrs. Simmons is married to folk-sculptor John-Paul Simmons who has exhibited at the Museum of American Folk Art. Mrs. Simmons lives in Hudson, New York, near the couple's daughter Natasha Simmons and grandchildren Damian Patrick Hall Simmons and Tamara Miquel Hall Simmons. John-Paul, who suffers from chronic schizophrenia, lives in a home for mental patients in Albany, New York. Mrs. Simmons occasionally visits long-time friends in Charleston, South Carolina.